AGGIES
OF THE PACIFIC WAR

New Mexico College of A & M
and the War with Japan

by
Walter Hines

Yucca Tree Press

First Printing   October 1999

Hines, Walter
    AGGIES OF THE PACIFIC WAR: New Mexico College of A&M and the War with Japan

        1. New Mexico A&M College - Alumni.   2. New Mexico State University - Alumni.   3. World War II, 1939-1945 - Pacific Theater.
    I. Walter Hines.   II. Title.

Library of Congress Catalog Card Number: 99-071426

ISBN: 1-881325-37-7

Cover design: Steve Matson and Art Sponagel

Dedication

In fond rememberance of
Miss Era Rentfrow
whose love, devotion, and service
to her alma mater and its students spanned six decades.
Her painstaking compilation of the 'War Books'
made this book possible.
To me, she will always be The Greatest Aggie!

1919

1940s

(Photos courtesy: NMSU Alumni Assoc.)

Acknowledgments

The following have permitted the use of excerpts and photographs.

Associated Press, quotation, p. 37.

Henry Holt, & Co., *Battle Report: Pacific War Middle Phase*, by Captain Walter Karig and Commander Eric Purdon, map, p. 42.

Little, Brown and Company, *American Caesar* by William Manchester, maps on pp. x, 14, 18, 20, 22, 53, 54, 130.

Mrs. Douglas MacArthur and the Gen. Douglas MacArthur Foundation for excerpts from *Reminiscences* by Gen. Douglas MacArthur, pp. 58, 105, 106, 143-44.

Jack Durio, photograph, p. 75.

Storm and Darlene Gerhart, photograph p. 82.

Jim Meadows, photograph, p. 76.

New Mexico Magazine, photographs p, 66.

New Mexico State University Alumni Association, photographs - pp. 63-87.

Bill Porter Family, letters - pp. 12-13, 28-29, 108, 142-43; photographs and illustrations - pp. 71, 89, 152.

Presidio Press, *Corregidor: The Rock Force Assault*, by E. M. Flanagan, p. 123-24.

Random House, *Peleliu: Tragic Triumph*, by Bill D. Ross - pp. 91-92, 95-96, 97, 98.

St. Martin's Press, *Hero of Bataan: The Story of General Jonathan M. Wainwright*, by Duane Schultz, p. 39.

St. Martin's Press, *Retaking the Philippines: America's Return to Corregidor and Bataan*, by William B. Breuer - pp. 118-19, 126-28.

Simon & Schuster, Inc., *Tales of the South Pacific*, by James Michener, p. 1.

Michael Taylor, "Aggies, Oh Aggies," p. 4.

Gerald Thomas, *Torpedo Squadron 4*, pp. 132-33; photograph, p. 74

US Army, photographs - pp. 73, 78-79, 82-85, 87-89

US Marine Corps, photograph - p. 86

US Navy, photographs - pp. 77, 79, 86, 88

Yucca Tree Press, *Heroes of Bataan, Corregidor, and Northern Luzon*, photographs - pp. 67-69, 85.
Beyond Courage by Dorothy Cave, pp. 9, 16-17, 33.

Table of Contents

List of Illustrations

FOREWORD

The mid-1990s witnessed a number of 50th anniversary ceremonies across America in remembrance of the great Allied victory over fascism and tyranny in World War II. One of the ceremonies, a symposium entitled, *Victory in World War II—The New Mexico Story*, was held at New Mexico State University in October 1993. Relatively ignorant of World War II history, I attended almost as an afterthought. I was going to Las Cruces for a NMSU Homecoming anyway, so why not arrive a day early and see what was to be learned.

At the symposium I was surprised, at age 50, to be one of the younger people in the audience. Where were the baby boomers, generations X'ers, and students? Was World War II already so distant a memory or eclipsed in importance by other events that few young people cared? Soon, such musings vanished as I listened to the colorful accounts and stories of the contributions made by New Mexicans during the War. There were Navajo Code talkers and survivors of the Bataan Death March. There were talks on the history of Los Alamos, White Sands and the atomic bomb. Author Dorothy Cave gave a stirring remembrance of the New Mexico National Guard's 200th Coast Artillery in the Philippines and the POW camps.

Ex-Aggies Henry Gustafson, Wilma Helen Strickland Hampton, and John Pershing Jolly described their amazing war adventures. Gustafson was a young Marine who survived the sinking of the carrier *USS Lexington* in the Battle of the Coral Sea and won the Silver Star for heroism during the Battle of Peleliu. Hampton was the first Aggie to join the newly formed Women's Army Corps. Jolly made a daring escape from a German POW train in Italy after being captured in North Africa.

Retired Professor Simon Kropp and Josephine Milton, widow of ex-President and General Hugh M. Milton, II, spoke of life on campus at New Mexico A&M during the War years. Near the end of the program, General Edward Baca gave a rousing account of the New Mexico National Guard's 120th Combat Engineers in Europe in which he mentioned my dad, the late Jerry Hines. Jerry, who was the athletic director (and football and basketball coach) at New Mexico A&M from 1929 to 1940, died in 1963 while I was a sophomore at NMSU. He had told me precious little about his own war experiences in Sicily and Italy. Mostly, he had spoken about his athletes—Pecos Finley, Jesse Mechem, and Ray McCorkle—each of whom died in the Philippines.

The day following the symposium, I went to the NMSU Alumni office to look through the multi-volume 'War Books' that had been mentioned by several speakers. The 'War Books' are really a series of scrapbooks—a compendium of lists, letters, photos, and newspaper clippings on Aggies in World War II. Long-time NMSU Registrar Era Rentfrow painstakingly compiled the 'War Books' as a labor of love. A Las Cruces native and 1919 graduate of New Mexico A&M, Era Rentfrow never married. But she was a surrogate mother to thousands of students during her tenure as Registrar from 1922 to 1963. As the Japanese rampaged through the Pacific and Asia in 1942, her 'boys' began dying and suffering in POW camps. Rentfrow was heartsick, but determined to document their stories and correspond with the families of the Aggies involved in the War.

By the time I left the Alumni office that day in October 1993, I wondered why no one had ever written a detailed article about Aggies in World War II. The stories were fascinating, the events richer than any war novel. I came back again the next day to pour over the 'War Books' in earnest. I made notes, recordings, took pictures, and crosschecked the names and faces with those in the old annuals also shelved in the Alumni office. I soon realized why no one had ever written an article on Aggies in WW II. It was too big an undertaking. A book would be required just to tell the story of the Aggies of the Pacific War. Aggies of the China-Burma and European Wars would have to wait.

Aggies of the Pacific War is based on information gleaned from the 'War Books,' by interviews, and archival research in Las Cruces, Santa Fe, and Washington, D.C.; and selected readings of military books dealing with U.S. forces in the Pacific. The intent is to weave the individual stories of Aggie soldiers, sailors, and airmen into a broader, overall picture of the Pacific War. Some of the individual stories are based on fragmentary information—sketchy newspaper clippings and second hand accounts. Although every effort was made to be as factual as possible, some stories are supplemented by my best inferences as to time, place, and circumstance. I apologize for any mistakes or inaccuracies. They are unintentional, but any mistakes are mine alone.

I know there are many more stories about Aggies in the Pacific War and wish it was possible to include them all. I apologize to those men and their families whose contributions are not mentioned here.

The initial mention of Aggie veterans in the text is accompanied by a citation (in parentheses) of hometown and graduation year, or year of last attendance. For example, the first mention of Jesse Mechem in Chapter 1 reads as Jesse Mechem (Las Cruces, '33). The back of the book includes an annotated list of known Aggies killed during World War II and a list of those Aggies who became Japanese POWs; many of them made the Bataan Death March.

I am very grateful to my wife Bettie for her support and patience. On many weekends, I woefully neglected my yard chores and other assigned duties while working on the manuscript. I was also fortunate to have Kennedy/Jenks Consultants of Las Vegas as an employer. Enduring my erratic work schedule, the company and Office Manager John Burkstaller, an NMSU alumnus, gave me the freedom and time needed to complete the book.

Over the last seven years, Winston Shillito of El Paso became a friend. Winston, a native of Brazito and a Las Cruces High graduate from the late '30s, grew up with several of the Aggies and other New Mexicans mentioned in the book. As a survivor of Bataan and the Japanese POW camps, he experienced the same horror, despair, and finally, the sweet elation of liberation. He was a great help with the Philippine history and with personal contacts for the interviews of veterans and family members.

Debbie Widger and staff of the NMSU Alumni Association were always cordial and helpful during the days I monopolized the 'Alumni Living Room' for notes, recordings, and photos from the 'War Books' and old annuals. And I am thankful to those who supplied valuable photos, letters, advice, and interviews—Orren Beaty of Vienna, VA, Gloria Hayner Shelly Campbell and Pat Campbell of Las Cruces, Larry Campbell of Rogersville, Tennessee, Dorothy Cave of Roswell, Bernice Corley of Las Cruces, Jack Durio of Las Cruces, Wilber Fite of San Antonio, TX, C. Quentin Ford of Las Cruces, Carl Freeman of Espanola, Anthony George of Riverside, CA, Storm and Darlene Gerhart of Broadview, NM, Henry Gustafson of Las Cruces, Janie Matson of Las Cruces, Alice McCorkle Thomas Gruver of Las Cruces, Jack Horne of Santa Fe, Otis Horton of Commerce, TX, Donald Jeffus of Seattle, John Johnson of Portales, Winnie Porter Price Marshall of El Paso, Pat McClernon of Las Cruces, Judge Edwin L. Mechem of Albuquerque, Walt Nations of Albuquerque, Bill and Asa Porter of Deming, Lemuel Pratt of Albuquerque, Mark Radoslovich of Albuquerque, Mel Ritchey of Hale Center, TX, Colonel Gerald P. Schurtz of Las Cruces, Mansil Scrivner of Lakewood, CO, Elnora Williams Wiley of Las Cruces, and Morris 'Pucker' Wood of Portales.

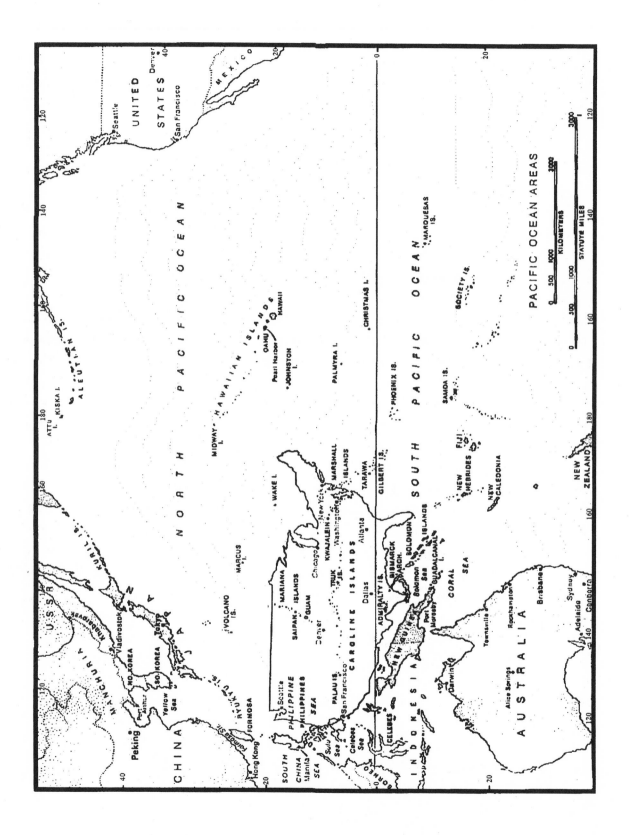

PRELUDE

They will live a long time, these men of the South Pacific. They had an American quality. They, like their victories, will be remembered as long as our generation lives. After that, like the men of the Confederacy, they will become strangers. Longer and longer shadows will obscure them, until their Guadalcanal sounds distant on the ear like Shiloh and Valley Forge. **J. Michener, Tales of the South Pacific.**

Records compiled by long-time New Mexico A&M registrar Era Rentfrow show that some 2,100 ex-students were in military uniform during WW II. At the time, this was fully a fifth of all those that had ever attended the college. They fought in all theatres of the War and dozens of key battles—Pearl Harbor, Bataan, Midway, Coral Sea, Guadalcanal, New Guinea, the Aleutians, the Philippines, Tarawa, Iwo Jima, Okinawa, Norway, North Africa, Sicily, Italy, France, Germany. More than 125 Aggies died. On a per capita basis, this was a casualty toll unmatched by any other non-military college.

Because of the school's long-established ROTC program, many of the dead were officers. And because of the role of ROTC and New Mexico's National Guard in bolstering the green Philippine Army before the surprise attack by the Japanese in December 1941, an inordinate number of Aggies fought in the Pacific War. Many became POWs after the fall of Bataan and Corregidor in spring 1942. Others were involved in the slow build up of U.S. forces in Australia, New Zealand, and the New Hebrides; and then, the arduous island hopping campaign against the Japanese throughout the Pacific.

The roll of Pacific Aggies included two New Mexico State Presidents—one sitting, Hugh Milton, and one future, Gerald Thomas. Both fought throughout the Pacific theatre and all the way to Japan, and both won medals for bravery. Others who fought in the Pacific included two of the college's all-time sports heroes, Pecos Finley (Causey, '39) and Jesse Mechem (Las Cruces, '33). And there were Ray McCorkle (Las Cruces, '32), Anthony

George (Gallup, '36), Louie Long (Portales, '39) and Morris 'Pucker' Wood (Portales, '39). Las Cruces favorite sons who entered the Pacific War in the early years included Henry Gustafson ('40), Charlie Sparks ('38), Francis Gallagher ('39), Wilber Fite ('40), Jack Durio ('41), Tom Esterbrook ('37) and William 'Wild Bill' Porter ('41). Others were the sons of famous families such as Jack Lee (Alamogordo, '41) and Albert Bacon Fall Chase (Three Rivers, '37).

These men, and hundreds of others, are the story of *Aggies of the Pacific War*. Many endured unbelievable hardships and suffering—the Bataan Death March, starvation and beatings in Japanese POW camps, nightmarish voyages to Japan on the Hell Ships, bloody battles on Guadalcanal, New Georgia, Bougainville, New Guinea, Kwajelein, Tarawa, Peleliu, Leyte, Luzon, Iwo Jima, and Okinawa. Others experienced the warm hospitality and comforts of wartime New Zealand and Australia, or made acquaintances with the friendly, exotic natives of the Solomons and New Guinea. Dozens, including Bill Porter, Jack Durio, Wilber Fite, and Henry Gustafson, won medals for heroism.

Many others fought and survived, or died, in the brutal island, sea, and air battles of the South and Central Pacific. Some, like Colonel Hugh Milton and Major James Gerhart (Santa Fe, '39), had the honor and satisfaction of helping to recapture the Philippines and liberate the POW camps of Manila. At least one, POW John Farley (Raton, '38?), was an eyewitness to the atomic bomb dropped on Nagasaki. A lucky few viewed the dramatic Japanese surrender on the battleship *Missouri* in Tokyo Bay presided over by General Douglas MacArthur. Engrossed in one of the epic events of human history, these young men from a small college in southern New Mexico experienced the totality of a desperate, brutal war the likes of which one hopes never to see again. Above all, the Aggie soldiers, sailors, and airmen, and their gallant families at home, did their duty and made the sacrifices to protect an America they loved.

The story of New Mexico State's Pacific Aggies actually began over 100 years ago with the founding of Las Cruces College as a land grant institution. Founded in 1889 under the leadership of Hiram Hadley, Las Cruces College soon evolved into the New Mexico Agricultural College under the Territorial Legislature's Rodey Act. Soon after, it became New Mexico College of Agriculture and Mechanic Arts (NM A&MA or NM A&M), and, finally, in 1959, New Mexico State University.

Under the Morrill Act signed into law by President Abraham Lincoln in 1862, a land grant institution like NM A&M was conceived as an educational beacon for the children of the "industrious classes." The "industrious classes" were, to put it simply, the working families of America. They manned the factories, the farms, the ranches, and the small businesses. And their sons and daughters needed a fair break at getting an education. Fittingly, as NM

A&M hit its stride in the '20s and '30s, its students came mostly from the rural and small town families of New Mexico and Texas.

The Morrill Act required the instruction of young men in "military science." The military science curricula led to a Reserve Officers Training Corps (ROTC) program at NM A&M in 1902. The ROTC program produced a number of Aggies who served in World War I, including ten who gave their lives. One of the dead was Joseph Quesenberry (Las Cruces, '16), star Aggie footballer whose sacrifice was later honored by the naming of Quesenberry Field adjacent to Williams Gym in the mid-1930s. Joe Quesenberry's nephew, James (Las Cruces, '41) was destined to die in World War II in air action over the South Pacific. Through WW I and until the time of WW II, the ROTC program at NM A&M was the only military program at New Mexico colleges; other than that at the two-year New Mexico Military Institute at Roswell. Thus, for young male students at NM A&M, part of the bargain was at least two years of service to Uncle Sam in mandatory military training in ROTC. Besides the class work, there were weekly drills on Miller Field, IG inspections, rifle cleaning sessions, and summer camps complete with mock combat exercises, rifle and artillery training, mules, horses, and cavalry charges. Despite the work and the discipline, the truth was that most didn't mind. ROTC provided camaraderie, a few extra dollars a month, and shoes and uniforms that, for want of a real wardrobe, some wore all week.

Perhaps the best known of the leaders of NM A&M's Military Science (ROTC) Department in the early years was Colonel Alexander Chilton. He served as Head of the Department from 1929 to 1934, at which time he became a Professor of English, though still serving as a special 'military advisor.' In 1940, as the country moved toward military mobilization, he once again took over and led the ROTC program through the crucial war years. An urbane soldier-scholar, Chilton had previously taught at West Point and was the author of an English textbook. He was a fine public speaker and loved the theater, taking an active part in many campus plays leading the 'Yucca Players.'

Chilton's right arm was the street-wise Irishman, Sergeant Jack 'Sarge' Cragin. A campus favorite, he would remain with the ROTC department through the war years. Cragin knew the military and how to teach discipline, but always came across as a friendly uncle. He bailed the boys out of scrapes, located part-time jobs, and had the connections to get young commissioned officers good assignments. He owned a farm within walking distance of campus just northeast of St. James Episcopal Church in Mesilla Park. Those who knew Cragin remember his smile, sparkling eyes, keen wit and insistence that on social occasions, as a 'friend of the shamrock.' you were expected to imbibe in his beloved 'Irish smile medicine.'

Many in ROTC during the 1930s, and others who opted out after two years without commissions, were also members of one of the two New Mexico National Guard units—the

111th Cavalry (which later became the 200th Coast Artillery) or the 120th Combat Engineers. Like ROTC, the Guard was all part of the fun and brought a little adventure and extra money for financially strapped Aggie students. Engineering Dean, and later President, Hugh Milton was active in the Guard, and led many Aggie cadets to summer camps at Fort Hood and Fort Bliss, Texas and Camp Luna near Las Vegas, NM.

By the mid-30s as the enrollment at NM A&M neared one thousand, ROTC had grown in size and popularity. However, as Michael Taylor (Hillsboro, '39) recalled in a wry memoir entitled, *Aggies, Oh Aggies*, some cadets did not take it as seriously as Chilton, Cragin, and the other instructors would have preferred.

> *Though by no means a pacifist, I had a suspicion, which proved well-founded, that I would make a so-so soldier. I did not like the uniforms, which seldom approximated a fit, and especially loathed the so-called overseas cap, which made most of us resemble organ grinders' companions. We drilled once a week, on Fridays as I recall, and the drill was the old-style "square" type, a complicated business involving in-place pivoting by some and mad rushes by others, to such orders as "squads right front into line." Our instructors were Colonel F. R. Waltz and Major A. J. MacNab (1935-37), and Colonel A. T. Fletcher and Major H.P. Hallowell (1937-39), with Staff Sergeant J. E. Cragin serving throughout (and for years before and after). The student battalion commanders were such stalwarts as Hugh Master, Jack Baird, Roscoe Peacock, William Chamberlin, and A. E. 'Steamboat' Baird.*
>
> *In my sophomore year I was promoted to corporal. Fortunately, all of my squad except one other chap and I, were in the battalion band, so I never had to exercise command. The two of us served throughout as "file closers" to other units. When my mandatory two years were over I thankfully gave up the military life and did not resume it until World War II.* [Taylor served as a Marine officer in the South Pacific].

Among those receiving commissions in the early Chilton/Cragin years were Jesse 'Jay' Mechem and the McCorkle twins, John Ray and Robert Roy (known as Ray and Roy). Mechem and the McCorkles won acclaim on the athletic field and in the classroom, besides being student leaders. Both Jesse Mechem and Ray McCorkle were Senior Class Presidents and were selected by their classmates as 'Greatest Aggies.'

The son of prominent Las Cruces attorney and mayor, Edwin Mechem, Jesse was a natural leader and an outstanding ROTC cadet. His younger brother, Ed and older brother Davenport, like Jesse, were Aggie athletes. Ed was destined to become a multi-term Governor of New Mexico in the 50s and 60s, a Senator, and a long-serving Federal District Judge in Albuquerque (as of 1999, he was still serving). Jesse starred in both football and basketball, winning All-Border Conference honors and taking special pleasure in Aggie victories over the Texas Miners and New Mexico Lobos. After graduation in 1933, Mechem went on to coach and teach at Las Cruces and Tucumcari High Schools. In 1937, he accepted a commission in the Army, training at Fort Huachuca, Arizona, before serving for two years in Hawaii just prior to the War. Mechem was then assigned to the newly formed 96th Infantry Division that was "built from scratch" and earmarked for duty in the Pacific. Mechem was destined to help lead MacArthur's "return to the Philippines" as commander of an infantry battalion in the 96th's 382nd Regiment. The 382nd was one of the first combat units to land on Leyte in October 1944.

Ray McCorkle, a civil engineering graduate and star football player, graduated in 1932. Poised to start a career and a family, he soon married Nellie Starr of Hatch, daughter of Arthur Starr, State Senator and New Mexico A&M Regent. Upon completion of his degree in 1932, McCorkle worked for the US Forest Service at Mayhill, New Mexico, and the U.S. Soil Conservation Service at Montrose, Colorado. He was commissioned and called to duty with the Army Air Corps in the Philippines in the summer of 1941. His air squadron was destroyed in the Japanese attack on Clark Field only a few hours after the Pearl Harbor attack. Unfazed, McCorkle took up the fight as an infantry commander on Bataan.

At a recent Homecoming, a former classmate recounted a campus incident involving McCorkle and a bully, a newly arrived Texan. Two weeks into the 1931-32 school year, the bully was parading around arrogantly, bragging about his amorous conquests and football exploits. Half the students were either disgusted or had been insulted. But the truth was that most were too intimidated to act. McCorkle, whose short stature and wire rimmed glasses belied a muscular build, had seen enough. One morning on the way to class, he spotted and approached the big bully outside Hadley Hall. McCorkle got in his face.

"We don't need your kind around here. I think you better give serious consideration to moving on," he said. The bully hesitated, made a fist, then thought better of tangling with McCorkle. His bluff called, the Texan withdrew without a fight and took McCorkle's advice. He was soon gone from campus.

In 1935, two of the new ROTC cadets were freshmen Pecos Finley (Causey, '39) and Morris 'Pucker' Wood (Portales, '39). Fresh off the Floyd Broncos state championship basketball team, Finley and Wood came to State College on athletic scholarships. Both were from rural farm families. Between 1936 and 1939, they teamed with Joe Jackson, Kiko Martinez, Mel Ritchey, and other boys of the "industrious class" to lead the Aggies to three Border Conference basketball championships and an NIT appearance in Madison Square Garden. Finley was elected Senior Class President in 1938-39. Michael Taylor recalled in

Aggies, Oh Aggies, that "Pecos was selected as Most Popular Boy in only one year, 1939; but, in fact, was our most popular through all his Aggie years."

Graduating in May 1939, Finley finished ROTC summer camp and returned to his first love, basketball. With ex-Aggie teammate Bob Sims (?TX, '39), he spent a year in the 'House of David' organization on a barnstorming semipro basketball team. Returning to Las Cruces in fall of 1940, Finley leased and operated the Texaco station on Main Street in Mesilla Park. His predecessor at the Texaco station was ex-classmate Tom Palmer (Albuquerque, '37). A trombone player with the Aggie marching band during his time at State College, Palmer didn't know that he would soon be meeting up with Finley again in the Philippines. Palmer would be with the 200th Coast Artillery Band and Finley with the Philippine Scout Quartermaster.

As 1941 dawned on Manila, there was growing anxiety about Japanese intentions in the Pacific. A number of ex-Aggie civilians, and many fellow New Mexicans, found themselves in precarious positions in the Philippines. William Trogstad (Las Vegas, '37) and James Rice (Las Cruces, '41) were working as mining engineers on Luzon with their wives. Neither knew what fate had in store. Rice would be captured and jailed by the Japanese at Baguio. Fortunately, his wife and three children had already fled to Pearl Harbor before the Japanese attacked the Philippines in December 1941. Trogstad's wife, Martha, was not so lucky. She was captured and incarcerated by the Japanese at Los Banos south of Manila while her husband fought on as an Army officer on Bataan.

With Martha at Los Banos was ex-Aggie George Gray (La Mesa, '32). Gray, whose brother Ed (La Mesa, '38) was later killed in naval action off Okinawa in 1945, was one of five Gray brothers who fought in WW II. George Gray was among a group of captured American officials who served in the office of the Philippine High Commissioner, Francis Sayre. When Manila fell in late 1941, Gray and Sayre's entire staff were captured and imprisoned (Sayre and family escaped from Corregidor by submarine). Three years later, an emaciated, brave George Gray would play a critical role in the brilliant military operation that liberated the Los Banos POW Camp in 1945.

John R. McFie, Jr. (Las Cruces, '05) was another ex-Aggie living in Manila in 1941. He was the son of the first President of the New Mexico A&M Board of Regents, John R. McFie, for whom the first permanent campus building had been dedicated in 1891. McFie, Jr. was a retired Lieutenant Commander in the Navy who had been in business in Manila for 25 years with his wife Dorothy. When Manila fell in late December 1941, the McFies were arrested by the Japanese and imprisoned with several thousand civilians at the converted Philippine University, Santo Tomas.

BUILD UP

As war clouds loomed over the new decade of the '40s, Aggies saw friends and ex-classmates enlist in New Mexico's 200th Coast Artillery. Others with ROTC commissions were being called to duty in the Philippines to fill specialty or leadership roles with Filipino units. Still others, like Henry Gustafson, Wilber Fite, and Tom Esterbrook were among a host of Aggies readying to fight in other areas of the Pacific.

Graduating in 1940 at age twenty with a ROTC commission, Gustafson was first offered a regular commission in the Army. But it was discovered that he was too young to meet Army rules. He went to Sarge Cragin for advice. Cragin suggested the Marines, since they were taking ROTC graduates at age twenty. Gustafson applied and was accepted. On June 30, 1940, he was sworn in at State College by Colonel Chilton. He traveled by train to Philadelphia for Marine Corps training with 128 other ROTC graduates from across the U.S. along with twenty-five graduates from the Naval Academy. After eight months of training, the Marine Corps must have thought Gustafson was a good salesman because his next assignment was as a recruiter. He spent three months touring college campuses, including stints at Texas Tech where he was 'taken in' by Dr. and Mrs. Harry Kent. Kent, a popular ex-President of NM A&M had known Gustafson as a student. He was presidential assistant at Tech at the time.

Henry had fun as a recruiter but decided he needed to see more of the world. In June 1941, he volunteered for the Pacific and was assigned to sea duty with the *USS Lexington* at Pearl Harbor, Hawaii. It was the start of an amazing adventure, harrowing escapes, and much glory for the young lieutenant. On Peleliu, as one of the youngest Majors in the Marine Corps, he would lead a batallion in a stunning amphibious assault against entrenched Japanese defenders, and win the Silver Star.

* * *

After graduation with a ROTC commission in 1940, Wilber Fite spent ninety days in training with the 23rd Infantry Division at Fort Sam Houston. Upon discharge from the Army, he went to work for Sears and Roebuck in El Paso. In summer 1942, Fite was called back to duty with the 96th Infantry Division. After initial formation at Camp Roberts in California, the 96th undertook training at rainy Camp Adair near Corvallis, Oregon. Despite the grey storm clouds, Fite was in good spirits. Because joining him with the 96th were some old friends—Aggies Jesse Mechem, Walt Nations (Arrey, '36), Carl Freeman (Carrizozo, '40), and Henry Medinger (Portales, '41). Nations would later be transferred to the European theatre. But the others would all see action together on Leyte and Okinawa. All would win medals for heroism.

Tom Esterbrook, was a party loving farm boy from La Mesa. A good athlete, Esterbrook was an Aggie basketball letterman on a team that won the Border Conference championship in 1937. He was a cadet officer in the ROTC program and received a commission in summer 1937. Following graduation, he spent several years working and playing semipro baseball on the West Coast. In 1941, Esterbrook joined the Army as a 1st Lieutenant and became an airborne soldier with the newly formed 503rd Parachute Infantry Regiment training at Fort Benning, Georgia. The 503rd, a tough and rowdy bunch, would become one of General MacArthur's favorite combat units in the Pacific.

As Gustafson, Fite, Esterbrook, and other Aggies began their military careers, the 200th Coast Artillery, with more than 1400 New Mexicans, was federalized and called to active duty in January 1941. The 200th was sent for training at Ft. Bliss under regimental commander, Colonel Charles Sage, publisher of the *Deming Headlight* in his civilian life. Among the 200th officers were Hubert Jeffus (Lordsburg, '35), Reynaldo Gonzales (Mora, '34), Anthony George (Gallup, '36), Dallas Thorpe (Artesia, '37), and Gerald Greeman (Deming, '40). Jeffus, an Aggie basketball letterman and cheerleader, had been a civil engineer working with the State Highway Department in Santa Fe. Gonzales, an agriculture major at NM A&M, had been serving as County Agricultural Extension Agent in Mora. George, ex-All Border Conference lineman on the 1936 Aggie Sun Bowl team had been with the Ford Motor Company in Gallup. Dallas Thorpe, a chemical engineering graduate, was employed by the potash industry in eastern New Mexico.

Gerald Greeman, with a degree in agriculture from A&M, was working as an agent for the Department of Agriculture and helping with the family ranch at Deming when he got word of the call up of the 200th. A personable young man, he was assigned as regimental personnel officer. Greeman was instrumental in shaping the character of the 200th–he thought it was important to make it fully New Mexican.

As recounted by Dorothy Cave in *Beyond Courage.*

> *From the original 750 men and officers they began to expand to a war-strength complement of 1,800. New Mexican volunteers flooding into Fort Bliss requested assignment to the 200th ... . They joined to beat the draft, to be with their friends, and to belong to the best ... . Harry Steen, originally slated for Fort Dix, wasn't sure just how it happened, but, after being told to pack his gear and move across the road, found himself with old friends in the regiment. Pepe Baldonado was reassigned in the same group. That was fine with him—his brother Juan was already there. The Marines had rejected Robert Williams because his teeth were crooked. The 200th welcomed him— he was a New Mexican, wasn't he? Myrl McBride, arriving with Indian friends from Acoma, was siphoned likewise. "Just a coincidence," he shrugged.*
>
> *Lieutenant Gerald Greeman could have told him better. As regimental personnel officer, Greeman got a weekly list of draftees. He took the senior personnel officer at the reception center to a few parties and won his favor. Soon Greeman had permission to fill the remaining ranks of the 200th with New Mexicans whenever possible. Greeman thought a homogeneous unit would be a stronger. In the 200th, everyone knew someone from his home-town battery. This homogeneity was one reason for the 200th's noted* esprit de corps.

After a rousing, tough, and party-filled training period at Fort Bliss, the 200th was ordered to the Philippines, arriving by ship in September 1941.

In January 1941, about the time the 200th was activated, ROTC graduate Pecos Finley volunteered for duty with the Army. In February, he was assigned as Second Lieutenant to Fort Lee, Virginia, with the 12th Quartermaster Training Regiment. Camp Lee, which had only recently been authorized for construction, was designated as the new training center for Army Quartermaster soldiers. Vast cadres of construction workers were still digging, hammering, and painting when Finley arrived. As had been the case everywhere, Finley quickly made a name for himself as a gentleman, leader, and athlete among the many new officers and men at Camp Lee. (An athletic field was named in his honor at Camp Lee following Finley's death in the Philippines.)

Finley completed training in July 1941, and was promoted to 1st Lieutenant. He then received orders to report to the Philippine Scouts headquartered at Fort McKinley in Manila. On the way west to disembark at San Francisco, he had a brief homecoming in eastern New Mexico with his mother, Ada Ralston, and family. A short time later, Finley left for San

Francisco by auto with long-time friend 'Pucker' Wood. Wood remembers doing most of the driving. When they arrived in San Francisco, the awestruck country boys did a little sight seeing before Finley's departure.

Because the Philippine Army was in desperate need of Quartermaster troops, Finley took the San Francisco-to-Manila flight on the China Clipper to save time. The Clipper, the massive 'flying boat' operated by Pan American Airways, was America's aviation lifeline to the Pacific. Wood, who would later see duty in the Solomons and Philippines as a 1st Lieutenant with the 43rd Infantry Division, waved farewell to his best friend in August 1941. It would be the last time they would see one another.

Four days later, on a bright August afternoon, the gleaming Clipper with Finley aboard was still lumbering westward over the azure waters of the Central Pacific. Since departing Treasure Island in San Francisco Bay, the Clipper had flown doggedly on, stopping for fuel and rest in Hawaii, Midway, Wake Island, and Guam. Now the journey was nearly over and the twenty passengers and crew were anxious. Inside, peering out one of the windows Pecos Finley looked just like what he was—a New Mexico country boy lost in the vast Pacific.

Earlier that morning, as the Clipper lifted off the waters near Guam, doubts had crept into Finley's mind. What would the Filipinos think of a green young officer giving them orders? Would there be war with the Japanese? How would I react to combat? Would I ever see New Mexico again? Troubling thoughts. But the throaty roar of the Clipper's big engines distracted him, and the doubts passed. Soon the Clipper was in rain squalls, then breaking back into sunlight, it cruised over a coral atoll with a sparkling turquoise lagoon. Three more hours and the easternmost Philippine islands came into view. In late afternoon, there appeared the dark green hills, lakes, and fertile farm country of Luzon. When Finley caught his first glance of the beautiful Capital City of Manila, he was dumbstruck. It truly was 'The Pearl of the Orient.'

The Clipper glided to a landing on Manila Bay, on waters made choppy by heavy ship traffic. Everywhere were native canoes, small barges, freighters, and ferries. The Clipper taxied toward the anchorage at the Cavite Naval Yard where were anchored several destroyers, an oiler, and a cruiser. Seeing the US Navy should have been comforting, but Pecos was no doubt uneasy. He had now witnessed the ominous preparations for war in a continuous line across the Pacific—thousands of soldiers and sailors in Hawaii, the frantic pace of building and fortification of airfields and harbors at Midway, Wake, and Guam. Now, as he arrived at Manila, he saw more of the same.

Finley's assignment in Manila was with the Quartermaster regiment of the Philippine Scouts. Unlike much of General MacArthur's rag-tag Philippine Army, the Scouts were well-trained, courageous infantrymen who would later come to be respected by the Japanese. In mid-1941, key positions in the Scouts were being filled by young American officers, many of whom were southwesterners and recent ROTC graduates—young men who were eager, "used to the heat," and "knew a little Spanish." It seemed a perfect match for Finley and other New Mexico Aggies like William 'Wild Bill' Porter, Albert Bacon Fall Chase, Charlie Sparks, and Neil 'Sleepy' Foster (Deming, '35). All had made their own Pacific crossings (by water) and were on duty at the Scouts' main base at Fort McKinley, just south of Manila.

Finley's arrival in Manila was soon followed by the arrival of many New Mexico compadres of the 200th Coast Artillery in September 1941. As they disembarked in Manila, they were cheered by their New Mexico friends and the Filipino children who yelled "Hi Ho Silver!" and "Hello Joe!" Ominously, a few also heard a taunt, "Hey Suckers!" But the taunt was soon forgotten. Optimism was running high among the untested young New Mexicans, and even among some of the older, wiser hands that should have known better. Japan was savaging Manchuria and China, and making other menacing moves throughout the Pacific. Their soldiers, sailors, and airmen were well trained and fanatically dedicated. Japanese weapons and technology, once antiquated, were now formidable. Still, General MacArthur had fooled himself into believing that he might have a viable fighting force capable of repelling a Japanese attack on Luzon.

On paper, MacArthur had a large army and massive stores of food and equipment. He had a fine group of senior officers, a cadre of eager young (if untested) junior officers, 20,000 American troops spread throughout the islands, and 12,000 Philippine Scouts. But MacArthur's Philippine Army was far from a potent force. There were tens of thousands of untrained, undisciplined Filipinos, most from the poor barrios and rural villages. They spoke dozens of different dialects and many understood little English. Most of the equipment, except for the formidable new B-17s recently sent by General Marshall, was of World War I vintage. Much of the WW I vintage ammunition was old and faulty. MacArthur's pleas for more troops, new equipment, and updated ammunition were met with reassurances from Roosevelt and Marshall that help would be forthcoming.

Thus, in the fall of 1941, the danger of the situation was not fully understood. Besides, the newly arrived Aggies and their fellow New Mexicans were having too much fun to worry a lot about war. They enjoyed exotic, bustling Manila with its spectacular, colorful sunsets and charming people. There was sailing on Manila Bay, spicy foods, casinos, jai-lai matches, cock fights, cold beer, and beautiful Filipino women. Aggie and other New Mexican officers renewed acquaintances at Fort McKinley and at the posh Army-Navy Club, a world class facility complete with bay-view verandas, swimming pools, servants, stateside radio broadcasts, live music and dancing.

Among the many Aggies frequenting the Army-Navy Club was Lieutenant Bill Porter, newly commissioned ROTC officer and fresh off the family farm in the Mesilla Valley. Assigned by the Scouts to the 91st Infantry Division, he was thrown into the frantic effort to train the green Filipino troops in modern warfare. Porter wrote to his parents, Mr. and Mrs. Asa Porter, on June 8, 1941.

Dear Folks:

At last I have an opportunity to write ... . I hope you got my first letter and amateur wire. The wire costs only 20 centavos (10 cents). You can send me 30 words for a dime if you can locate an amateur station in El Paso.

Manila is nothing like an American city, but a lot like Juarez; if the adobe houses of Juarez were nepa shacks it would be very similar ... a nepa shack is very neatly woven of nepa (palm thatch) ... . The enormous windows are covered with nepa hatches when it rains. There must be 10,000,000 of these shacks in Manila. They may stand right beside a fine new building ... as if they belonged there. These people go in for ultra modern stuff; the only decent, conventional styled buildings being the Army-Navy Club (colonial), the Manila Hotel (looks like White House in El Paso) and about two or three office buildings. The streets are unpaved, dirty, twisting, unlighted, and muddy. The nepa shacks have spaced flooring and thru these spaces the wastes of all kinds are dropped, and there visit the family hog, dog, and rooster. There is a slaughterhouse right in the center of town (an open shed is all) where pigs squeal all night. The modern buildings are the Jai-Alai, several apartments, and gaming houses ... . The theaters are large, beautiful, and ultra modern with round mirrors and winding stairs. Everybody of class sits upstairs where you pay 1 peso for a seat. The government owns everything—theaters, Jai alai, gambling, hotels, and even calezos (pony drawn carts) which are painted every conceivable color in intricate designs. The ponies are much smaller than shetlands, skinny, hung all over with bells and shinny brass ... they are always kept at a trot; there must be no end to them, they are everywhere.

I got back from maneuvers and immediately left on a reconnaissance of the Lingayen Gulf area (our defense sector). Everywhere you saw tremendous old Spanish churches built of stone, and rapidly falling into decay, trees growing out of the bell towers ... they must have been beautiful in their day. The little towns or "barrios" have a market place just like Juarez, and sell the same things in the same way, and look like the same people. The country up here is very low, filled with tidewater rivers, swamps, rice paddies, and jungle. I went swimming in the Gulf and the water was so warm that it actually sapped [my] strength. The beach was tropically beautiful with tall coconut palms leaning over the water ... thousands of them. I've drunk all the coconut milk I'll ever want. This is where the Chinese pirates and Moros used to raise such havoc. The people still show the Chinese influence.

Until a bull carabao has stared at you, you haven't been stared at! That is the main reason we carry arms everywhere we go. They are black, tremendous, and their horns reach as much as seven feet. They are very pot bellied, short legged, with big soft looking feet (for mud). When they plod along they have a squishy, squashy rolling movement. They go crazy if kept away from water, and when not crazy I think they wish it would dry up so they could go crazy and kill somebody. But still you see 5-year olds kick them around. Just before I got here my platoon was attacked by one. Lt. Dosh fired eight rounds into him and still couldn't kill him. It's still alive, run off somewhere.

I went to Manila Polo Club [to watch his commanding officer play polo] *... I rode down there, but my boots have grown too small in the leg, so I had to wear my heeled boots. Everybody crowded around, so I had to ride for them in "Spanish style" ... it went over pretty big.*

There's a lot more fraternizing among officers here now that the women are gone, and some of these meek birds have turned out to be lions. Since I've been here, there have been two trials for "conduct unbecoming an officer." Also, innumerable reprimands.

I live in a twelve room house, with verandas and porches all around— great windows, latticed with a translucent sea shell filler, very tropical looking ... . We have two lavanderos and a No. 1 boy who cooks and cleans. The Lavanderos get 10 centavos a day ... .

I don't believe the Jap will fight, but if he does, heaven help us. These Geek soldiers [Filipinos] ... speak very little English, and are so excitable that if you shout a command they don't understand they immediately get stiff, close their minds like a door, and just say "yes sir, yes sir". If you say "commence firing" they may just sit down, close their minds, and drift away on a rose colored cloud ... . A white officer is a God ... a superior being ... .

I love you and all my thoughts are with you. Oh yeah, Father Braun from Mescalero is here and I will call next week ... .

Your devoted son,
Bill

WAR — THE PHILIPPINES

By fall 1941, the fun of Manila had given way to unease. MacArthur's forces, including Porter's 91st Division, held mock invasion exercises on the Lingayen Gulf and the lowlands leading south toward Manila. Charlie Sparks' 41st Division held maneuvers and began building defensive positions south of Manila. The 200th set up anti-aircraft positions around Clark Field and Ft. Stotsenberg. Pecos Finley's Quartermaster regiment hurriedly placed stores of food, ammunition, and equipment at assigned depots north and west of Manila.

MacArthur surmised that, if it came, the main Japanese attack would be by way of Lingayen Gulf and across the 120 miles of lowlands leading south to Manila. The mistake was in thinking his Philippine Army would be ready to take on the Japanese on the beaches and the plains. He thought the attack would be no sooner than spring 1942, and by then, defensive positions would be greatly strengthened.

The treacherous Japanese had other ideas. Following a final diplomatic breakdown with the Franklin Roosevelt administration, brought about largely by devious militant elements controlled by General Hideki Tojo, the Japanese implemented a series of previously planned surprise attacks on America's Pacific forces. Reluctantly, the brilliant Japanese Admiral Isoroku Yamamoto gave in to the war fever and joined in the operations. His first master stroke at Pearl Harbor, would be, as Roosevelt termed it, "a date that will live in infamy."

Early on the morning of December 7, 1941, a powerful Japanese carrier task force struck Pearl Harbor with bombers, Zeros, and midget submarines. The surprise was so total that passengers on an incoming American liner were pleased to witness what they thought was a remarkably realistic U.S. military exercise. Aggie Leo Eminger (Portales, '40) was the navigator on a B-17 that arrived from the mainland during the attack. Eminger's plane landed amidst the chaos and destruction of Hickam Field. The Japanese blasted Scofield Barracks and other military targets, but saved their real savagery for Pearl Harbor where the U.S.

warships lay placidly at anchor, conveniently lined up in rows. They sank or seriously damaged six great battleships—*Arizona, Nevada, West Virginia, California, Tennessee*, and *Oklahoma*. But miraculously, no aircraft carriers were hit. The US Navy had only four at the time, and none was at Pearl Harbor.

On one of these carriers, the *Lexington*, was young Marine Lieutenant Henry Gustafson. The *Lexington* had left Pearl on December 5th to deliver planes to Midway. When the *Lexington* returned on December 12th, Gustafson was witness to the devastation wrought by the Japanese. The American battleship fleet had been nearly wiped out, and more than 2,100 sailors and soldiers were dead. Scores of American warplanes had been totally destroyed. Japanese radio bragged that the United States had been "reduced to a third-rate power."

News of the Pearl Harbor debacle was several hours late in coming to MacArthur in Manila. When he got the news there was a brief period of disbelief. MacAruthur's staff thought the Pearl Harbor damage had been exaggerated. American intelligence still was not convinced that a Japanese attack on the Philippines was imminent.

On Formosa, where the Japanese had massed their planes for an attack of Luzon, the Emperor's airmen fidgeted and worried. They were socked in by fog. Believing that the attack on Pearl Harbor was common knowledge, they were sure the Filamericans would be alert and waiting. Fortunately for the Japanese, the weather cleared, and their aircraft were soon airborne.

The huge force of Japanese bombers and Zeros attacked Clark Field at noon on December 8, 1941. Because of the international dateline, it was acually the same day as the Pearl Harbor attack. Incredibly, the newly arrived B-17s and a squadron of P-40s, loaded with bombs and 50-caliber machine guns, were parked on the runway in neat rows—the proverbial sitting ducks. The American pilots were inside having a leisurely lunch. The Clark Field radar system was not operating properly, so the Japanese attack was a complete surprise, and literally destroyed MacArthur's Philippine Air Force on the ground.

Around Clark, the New Mexicans manning the anti-aircraft guns sprung into action. The 200th's old WW I anti-aircraft guns downed several Japanese planes. But the gunners cursed a storm when they discovered that more than half their ammunition was duds, and that much of the rest was improperly fused. Most of their shots exploded harmlessly hundreds of feet below the Japanese planes. Ray McCorkle with the 4th Air Base Group at Clark, was among those who experienced the fury of the surprise attack. The attack left McCorkle and the 200th defenders at Clark Field dazed, bleeding, or both. Dorothy Cave's book, *Beyond Courage*, described the scene.

The burning field seemed strangely quiet...except for sudden explosions,
and wounded horses screaming in agony ... suddenly strains of music wafted

through the air ... . "The old gray mare, she ain't what she used to be, ain't what she used to be ... ."

Led by their jaunty warrant officer Jim McCahon of Albuquerque, ex-Aggie Band trombonist Sergeant Tom Palmer and the 200th band came playing and marching down the runway. The music brought a surreal levity to the disaster. Wry smiles appeared on the faces of the dazed troops. But then a plane appeared over the field. It looked like a Zero. Spooked, the band members dropped their instruments and made for the ditches, firing their rifles. The 'Zero' was actually an American P-40, shot up and staggering back to base. As the P-40 made a shaky landing on the cratered runway, the 200th band got up, dusted themselves off, reslung their rifles, and coolly resumed playing and marching down the runway. Despite the distraction of the music, the New Mexicans and other Clark defenders were left frustrated and shaken by their first encounter with the pilots of the 'Rising Sun.'

And soon it would get worse. Within a few days, the Japanese began the land invasion of Luzon under the command of Lieutenant General Masaharu Homma. They struck first 200 miles north of Manila with minor landings at Aparri and Vigan. Then on December 12th Homma's troops landed at Legaspi, 150 miles southeast of Manila. Every day, the Japanese planes bombed and strafed at will, meeting little challenge from the few remaining American planes. The 200th continued to fight the Japanese planes attacking Clark Field. A portion of the regiment was designated as the 515th Coast Artillery and hastily moved to Manila to provide more anti-aircraft protection around the harbor.

Bill Porter and the 91st Division, along with the 11th and 21st Divisions and General Jonathan 'Skinny' Wainwright's beloved 26th Cavalry, were rushed to defensive positions in the Lingayen lowlands. MacArthur had correctly surmised that this would be the location of the main invasion. A large Japanese landing force came ashore at Lingayen Gulf near Agoo on December 21st. Many in General Homma's force had been battle hardened in the recent Malaysian campaign against the British. They met spirited resistance for awhile, but with inadequate artillery and virtually no air support, the Filamerican forces in the Lingayen area were hard pressed to hold their lines.

Early in the battle near San Fernando, a Philippine infantry battalion was flanked by the Japanese and separated from its division, the 71st. They were forced to take to the hills and then tried to retreat south down the road to Baguio and on to Manila. Wainwright got word of the budding disaster, and Bill Porter and the 91st Infantry's Regimental Combat team were rushed to the scene to bolster the isolated 71st. Porter's exploits were described on a 'War Gum' trading card (see pg. 71).

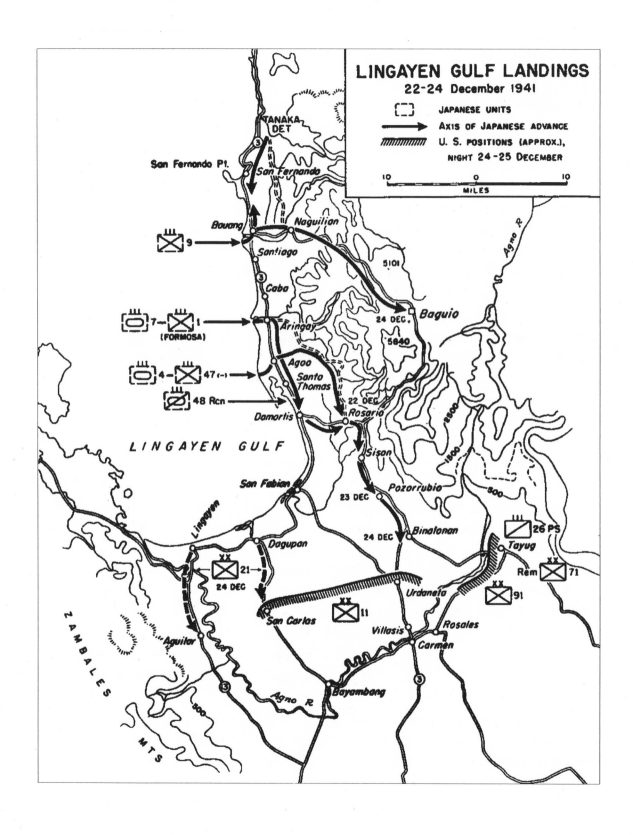

LINGAYEN GULF LANDINGS
22-24 December 1941

JAPANESE UNITS
AXIS OF JAPANESE ADVANCE
U. S. POSITIONS (APPROX.),
NIGHT 24-25 DECEMBER

An orderly withdrawal was made possible by a Lieutenant William Por-
ter of New Mexico, a "second Sergeant York," who, rifle at shoulder, crouched
at the end of a bridge and coolly picked off one by one a Japanese unit
manning a machine gun nest. The enemy steadily pumped lead at him and
the battle-weary Filipinos but he pulled the trigger until the last of the Japs
was gone and their fire was silent. The battalion then circled enemy posi-
tions and got back to its post.

As the Filamericans staggered back across the lowlands towards Manila, MacArthur activated the 'Orange Plan,' a strategy for a five-stage delaying action by fighting retreat into the natural fortress of Bataan. A mountainous, densely vegetated peninsula across Manila Bay from the Capital City, Bataan was protected by Corregidor—a small volcanic island bristling with guns and tunneled fortifications a few miles off the southern tip of Bataan at the approach to Manila Bay. MacArthur's headquarters were in Malinta Tunnel deep inside the mountains of Corregidor.

With the retreat in full swing, Pecos Finley and the Scout quartermaster troops were faced with salvaging as much of the misplaced stores as possible. What couldn't be loaded and trucked or boated to Bataan and Corregidor was to be destroyed. But, too little of either occurred. The Japanese were advancing too fast. The logistics of moving the supplies and equipment was a full-blown nightmare. Military vehicles were in short supply and senseless arguments abounded with Filipino businessmen and authorities over payment for buses and trucks and who would man the warehouses and loading operations. There was the asinine situation of Filipino laws that forbid rice from being moved from one province to another. Desperate back-and-forth runs were made along the clogged narrow roads leading to Manila in a last ditch effort to bring supplies to Bataan.

Because of the inability to move the huge rice stores from Cabanatuan, north of Manila, a two-year supply of rice for 100,000 men was wasted. Incredibly, the rice simply fell into the hands of the advancing Japanese. Later, at Bataan, the food could have averted wide-spread famine among the weakened, ill Filamerican defenders. Bataan had been stocked with only a thirty-day supply of skimpy field rations for the 15,000 American and 50,000 Filipino troops. To make matters worse, 25,000 civilian refugees streamed into Bataan. They too needed to be fed.

As the situation deteriorated, Manila was declared an 'open city' by MacArthur on December 26th to avert civilian slaughter. But the Japanese continued to bomb and shell the city. Some believed it was the Japanese way of punishing the Filipinos for siding with the Americans.

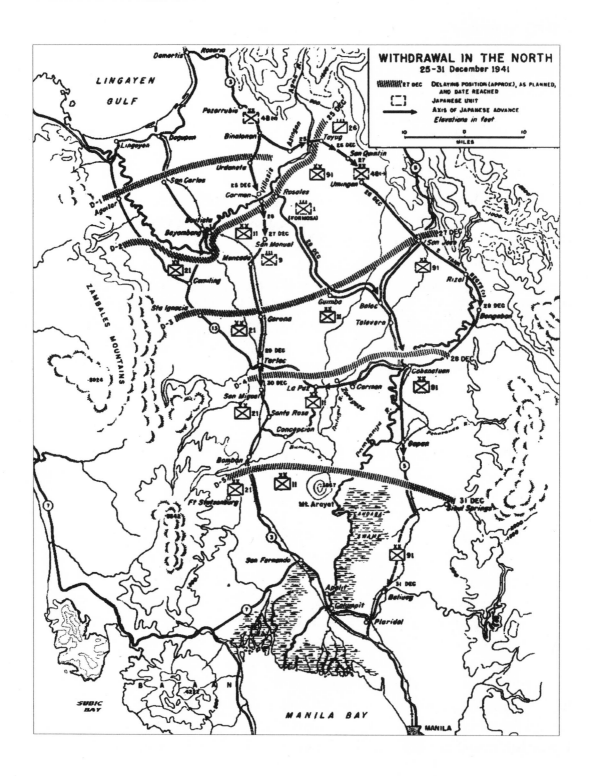

Meanwhile, under the leadership of General Wainwright, the Filamericans north of Manila fought a brilliant delaying action over a two-week period, falling back in a series of predetermined lines to defensive positions along rivers and other natural barriers. The 200th was called upon to defend the key bridges leading to Bataan, which were blown in a masterful fashion just as the retreating Filamericans crossed ahead of the Japanese.

On New Year's Day, 1942, the last critical bridges leading to Bataan still stood, at Calumpit on the Papanga River, and Layac Junction on the Culo River. As soldiers, civilians, buses, trucks, carts, and animals streamed across, the battle hung in the balance. The retreating Filamerican units, the 11th, 21st, 71st and 91st Divisions from the north and the 41st (with Charlie Sparks) and the 51st Divisions from the south, had to make it across the Calumpit Bridge before the Japanese. Then the Layac Bridge had to hold to allow all Filamerican forces to retreat into Bataan. Failure to hold the bridges long enough meant envelopment and annihilation.

Once again, Lieutenant Bill Porter was called upon to lead an exhausted unit of 91st Division troops to defend a key bridge, this time the Calumpit. The bridge was rigged to blow, but the retreating Filamerican divisions from the south were late. Anxious hours passed as Wainwright wrung his hands and worried, calling frantically for information on the whereabouts of the southern force. Suddenly, Japanese infantrymen appeared on the north side of the Papanga just about the time the retreating Filamerican units were sighted approaching the bridge. Porter's unit came under heavy fire, but they gave back worse than they got. The Aggies' 'second Sergeant York' was at it again, deftly picking off the Japanese on the far side of the river. The bridge held and the last Filamerican units made it safely across, whereupon it was destroyed in a thunderous blast.

Porter and his men had joined the retreat towards Bataan when someone realized that one of the unit's men was not with them. Porter commandered a jeep and sped back toward the Calumpit Bridge. As he approached, the enraged Japanese opened up. Porter spotted the wounded soldier and quickly loaded him into the jeep and sped off in a cloud of dust, smoke, and bullets. Somehow, Porter made it safely back to the retreating Filamerican column moving south. He appeared grinning, his jeep riddled with bullet holes. For his gallantry at Calumpit, 'Wild Bill' Porter would be awarded the Silver Star, the first New Mexico Aggie of WW II to be so honored. He was soon promoted to Captain.

Shortly after destruction of the Calumpit Bridge, the bridge at Layac was blown with the 200th providing final guard. Now the hungry, exhausted men thankfully retreated into the relative safety of Bataan. But they received bad news. MacArthur ordered his forces to endure half rations just as a confident enemy was joining The Battle of Bataan.

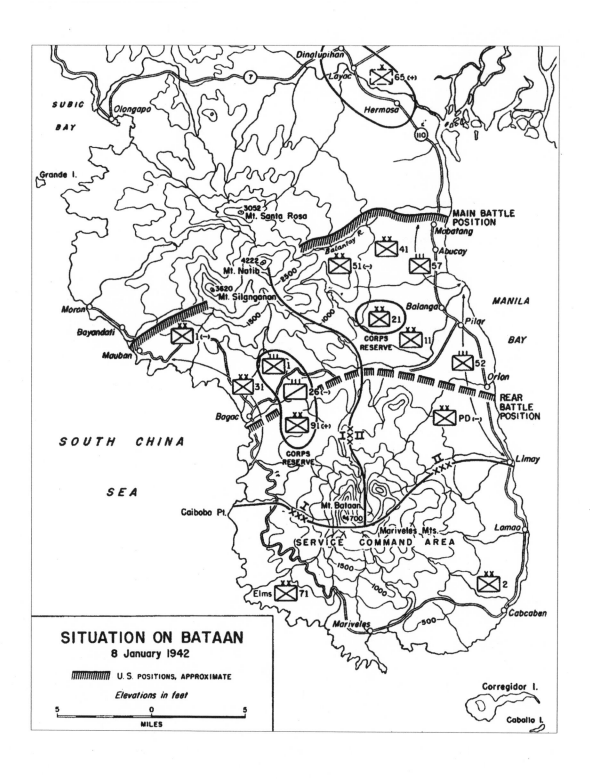

Dinalupihan

Layac

65 (+)

Hermosa

7

SUBIC
BAY

Olongapo

110

Grande I.

3052
Mt. Santa Rosa

MAIN BATTLE
POSITION

Mabatang

Balantay R.

41

Abucay

4222
Mt. Natib

51 (−)

57

3620
Mt. Silnganon

2500

MANILA

Balanga

Moron

2000

21

1500

Bayandati

1000

CORPS
RESERVE

11

BAY

Pilar

1 (−)

Mauban

31

1

Orion

52

26 (−)

Bagac

91 (+)

I
II

REAR
BATTLE
POSITION

SOUTH   CHINA

CORPS
RESERVE

PD (−)

II

SEA

Limay

Calbobo Pt.

I

Mt. Bataan
4700

Mariveles Mts.

Lamao

SERVICE   COMMAND   AREA

1500

1000

Elms

71

2

500

Cabcaben

Mariveles

SITUATION ON BATAAN
8 January 1942

|||||||||||| U.S. POSITIONS, APPROXIMATE

Elevations in feet

5   0   5

MILES

Corregidor I.

Caballo I.

THE BATTLE OF BATAAN

MacArthur's Orange Plan divided the peninsula of Bataan into two military sectors for defensive purposes. I Corps on the westside was under the command of General Wainwright. Brigadier General George Parker commanded II Corps on the east. A volcanic ridge that ran almost the entire length of Bataan separated the two sectors. Prominent mountains, Silanganan, Natib, and Mount Mariveles punctuated the ridge. Considered impassable to military units, the upper flanks and tops of the mountains were not defended by the Filamericans. The I Corp and II Corps sectors were bounded by Manila Bay on the east, and Subic Bay on the west.

The 41st Infantry and Captain Charlie Sparks took up positions in II Corps near Abucay on the first main line of resistance, the Mauban-Abucay Line across the northern part of Bataan. Captain Porter's unit of the 91st Division took up reserve positions in I Corps near Bagac, some 15 miles south of the Mauban-Abucay Line. The 200th was assigned to defend coastal hilltops and the tiny Bataan, Cabcaben, and Mariveles airstrips at the southern end of Bataan.

MacArthur's command staff, wife, and son Arthur were on Corregidor with a sizeable force of artillerymen, Marines, and quartermaster troops. With them were High Commissioner Frances Sayre and his wife, and Colonel Carlos Romulo whose 'Voice of Freedom' broadcasts to the Bataan defenders infuriated the Japanese. Corregidor had vast stores of ammunition, considerable food, and its own water supply.

Besides the infantry and artillery forces on Bataan and Corregidor, MacArthur had precious few other military resources. The 'Bataan Air Force' consisted of ten worn P-40s and a hodge-podge of old non-military planes known as the 'Bamboo Fleet.' The 'Bamboo Fleet' operated out of Bataan Field, and was soon infamous for its many daring medical, supply, and VIP runs to Panay, Mindanao and other southern islands. Short of fuel and parts and grossly overmatched by the large Japanese air force, the 'Fleet's' P-40s were used sparingly. But their brave pilots were able to inflict severe punishment on the Japanese during critical phases of battle. One of the pilots, Captain Ed Dyess, would later make an electrifying escape from the Japanese POW camp at Davao, Mindano, and bear the first eyewitness account of the Bataan Death March and other atrocities.

After the withdrawal of U.S. naval forces from Manila Bay in January 1942, MacArthur was left with little naval firepower. The 'Bataan Navy' included five PT-boats, two Q-boats (British PT-type boats) three minesweepers, three river gunboats, one sub tender, and two civilian motor boats that had been converted into patrol craft. The quick, maneuverable PTs came to be feared by the Japanese for their stealth and wallop. As described later, they played a key role in beating back early Japanese landing attempts on the west (I Corps) side of Bataan.

The sub tender *Canopus* docked on the southern tip of Bataan at Mariveles on December 29, 1941. The Japanese immediately attacked by air, and several direct hits by 250-pound bombs appeared to sink her. Actually, the *Canopus* was only grounded on the shallow bottom. Though listing she was only partly sunk. The Japanese considered the Canopus to be out of commission and of no military value, so they stopped bombing. It was a Godsend to the Bataan defenders. The clever sailors kept the *Canopus's* wonderfully equipped machine shops running at night, fixing everything the Army brought in and making many other things. A reservation system was devised and a steady stream of nurses, officers, and men came on board the *Canopus* in shifts to sample precious luxuries: ice cream, candy, cigarettes, hot showers, and hot meals served on linen tablecloths with homemade bread and butter.

As the *Canopus* did its duty, the Japanese were readying for ground action on Bataan. General Homma massed his troops and approached northern Bataan in early January 1942. The troops were cocky from their initial successes on Luzon and considered the Filamericans to be cowards running from an honorable fight. Homma was somewhat fooled and not sufficiently aware of the natural defensive terrain of Bataan. Nor did he fully recognize the strategic importance of the peninsula and Corregidor as to their command of Manila Bay. MacArthur was fond of saying, "They may have the bottle. But we still have the cork."

With the military situation going better than expected, Homma received orders from Imperial Headquarters on January 2, 1942. He was stunned. Homma was told to transfer his crack veteran troops of the 48th Division that had performed so well on Luzon. They would be used to move up General Tojo's schedule for the invasion of the Dutch East Indies. The Japanese needed the Indies' coveted oil supply. The 15,000 troops of the Japanese 48th were replaced with 6,600 green troops of the 65th Brigade. Many of these troops were in their 30s and 40s. The gallant Filamericans would soon teach the 'old men' of the 65th a lesson in humility.

The Japanese attacked Bataan by air and artillery bombardment in early January, followed by a series of coordinated infantry attacks. With fortified, well-entrenched positions, the Filamericans put up a tenacious defense. As defensive positions faltered or were outflanked, Generals Parker and Wainwright rushed reserves in to breach the gaps. MacArthur had ordered a strategy for a defense in depth, and it was working.

Frustrated by their inability to overrun the defenses, the Japanese resorted to fanatical measures. They infiltrated through the jungle at night. They slithered on their bellies for hours and knifed Filamerican defenders in their trenches. With green colored faces, camouflage suits, and special rifles, the snipers tied themselves to trees and wreaked havoc behind the Filamerican lines. They tried banzai charges and were slaughtered mercilessly by Filamerican automatic weapons fire. One charge by the Japanese in Charlie Sparks' 41st Division line of II Corps got hung up on parallel strings of barbed wire. The 41st soldiers came out of their foxholes and annihilated the Japanese, stabbing and slashing with their bayonets. In the morning, dozens of Japanese hung bleeding, moaning, and dead on the wire.

In desperation, Homma ordered ill-conceived, nighttime amphibious landings behind Filamerican lines along the western shoreline of Bataan in mid- and late-January. These actions became known as the Battle of the Points. One battle at Canas Point involved swashbuckling PT boat commander, Bill Bulkeley, the hero of MacArthur's subsequent escape from Corregidor. Bulkeley's PT boats led an attack on the slow-moving Japanese landing barges that had been detected in the moonlight. Concentrated fire from the PT's, coordinated with fire from a mixed group of Filamerican soldiers, airmen, cooks, and quartermaster troops on shore, killed hundreds of the hapless Japanese. The barges ran red with Japanese blood. But many still made it ashore and hung on doggedly for days. Finally, starving and dying of thirst and with defeat inevitable, the Japanese took suicide leaps off the cliffs into the ocean rather than surrender.

Meanwhile, a series of infantry and artillery battles were raging on land. The Japanese forces in II Corps (east side) finally broke through the 51st Division defenses on January 13, 1942, forcing a temporary pull back of the main line in that sector. A week later, a company of Japanese commandos, in a feat thought impossible, traversed Mt. Silanganan on the I Corps (west side) and temporally took over the coast highway before being routed by reinforcements. But relentless Japanese pressure, supported by artillery and bombs, finally wore down the battle-weary Filamericans. MacArthur ordered a withdrawal to the second line of defense, the Bagac-Orion Line.

In mid-January the Japanese made other amphibious landings along the western shore of Bataan. Although beaten back and eventually annihilated, the enemy fought to the last man and inflicted heavy casualties on the Filamericans. In another incredible testament to stamina and determination, a company of Japanese infiltrated over Mt. Nabib in the center of Bataan, and set up defenses in a dense, thicketed area. They held out for weeks in what became known as the Battle of the Pockets. Many non-infantry troops, including those from the grounded air corps, were thrown into these frays. Based on the available evidence it was probably in one of these battles where Ray McCorkle saw his last action.

After the debacle at Clark Field and the destruction of his air group, McCorkle was placed in command a company of 'infantry' made up of ex-Air Corps personnel, mechanics, and others without infantry training. On Christmas Eve, McCorkle's company had been moved by ship from Manila to Bataan where they were assigned a rear guard mission. Their orders were to hold their ground and give the main force of Filamerican defenders an opportunity to dig in further back along the Mauban-Abucay line. During this time, McCorkle's men successfully harassed Japanese patrols assigned to recon the Filamerican lines prior to the first big enemy attack in early January 1942.

McCorkle had previously distinguished himself in action at Clark Field and in Manila against strafing Japanese planes. According to a statement by a Major Mark H. Wohlfeld, executive officer of McCorkle's battalion

> *When the Japs began strafing ... Captain McCorkle joined the men in the foxholes firing at the planes. Miraculously, he escaped death as others fell around him. He would stand and fire as long as the planes remained within range ... . When he ran out of ammunition, he would take bullets from a dead companion.*

On Bataan, McCorkle's company, comprised mostly of Filipinos, was proving poorly disciplined and panicky in the face of the hardened Japanese troops. On January 28, the Japanese began penetrating the Filamerican lines. McCorkle's company was ordered to form a combat patrol and move forward. He decided to lead his men personally.

They moved down a draw under cover to a point near a small village that was infested with the enemy. McCorkle ordered an attack, but the men balked. He grabbed a supply of hand grenades and ordered the men to follow. He charged forward firing and throwing grenades. Suddenly, two hidden Japanese arose from the ground and fired. The first was shot dead by McCorkle. The other opened fire with a machine gun. The Captain was hit, fell, got up, and was hit again. Sergeant Fisher attempted to drag his commander back by the feet, but he too was hit and fell. Finally, another man in the company was able to drag McCorkle back to a ditch. He was covered with dirt and blood, wounded in the groin and the side of the head. He tried to get up. "Wipe this damned blood out of my eyes and let me back at 'em," he begged. But McCorkle was unable to stand and soon lapsed into unconsciousness.

He was carried back to an aid station and then to a field hospital in the rear. Without dog tags and separated from his little-known company, he was delirious and lay unconscious and unidentified for two days. On January 30 he regained consciousness briefly, long enough to identify himself. He collapsed again and died a few moments later.

News of McCorkle's death shocked Las Cruces where his parents lived and wife, Nellie Starr McCorkle, was a student at the College. Many classmates and teachers fondly remembered McCorkle. Daniel B. 'Dad' Jett, his former civil engineering professor wrote a glowing tribute. His sister, Alice Thomas (Gruver) penned a eulogy in the *Chaparral*.

> *There will never be another Ray McCorkle. His brief three decades are finished ... . My brother had the most beautiful character of anyone I have ever known. His only fault was an overzealous defense of the weak and under privledged. Many a time as children he made me thoroughly ashamed of a selfish thought or an uncharitable deed. All it took was a look from his honest grey eyes ... . He had high ideals and he lived up to them.*

Although Pilot H.G. Gilbert (Pennsylvania, '39), killed over Burma on December 23, 1941 was the first Aggie to die in the War, the memories of McCorkle and his sister's eulogy galvanized Las Cruces and State College. McCorkle was a bona fide hero and his death made the War real and frightening to those at home.

As if prodded by McCorkle's death, President Hugh Milton, who would shortly leave for active duty in the Pacific, announced that 500 Army recruits would soon come to NM A&M for training. It was the harbinger of a new program, the 'Army Specialized Training Corps.' A few months later, in summer 1942, 300 naval trainees came to campus and were housed in abandoned Civilian Conservation Corps camps. 'Dad' Jett of the Engineering school had already instigated a pilot training course for Aggie students on an airfield east of Las Cruces near Organ. Jack Durio (Las Cruces, '41) was among an early group that graduated from 'Jett's Air Force' to undertake further training in California and Corpus Cristi. Many, like Durio, would become Naval and Army aviators, navigators, or bombardiers.

Soon enrollment at NM A&M dropped dramatically. As the war news worsened and morale sank, Professor Gwynne L. 'Gus' Guthrie began a series of 'Radio War Talks' over the campus radio station, KOB. President Milton, a gifted orator, spoke publicly about how the Axis powers had underestimated the fighting will of America. "Insufficient manpower" led to the cancellation of intercollegiate athletics. The New Mexico College of Agriculture & Mechanic Arts was on a full war footing.

*　　*　　*

Meanwhile, the battle for the Phillipines raged. By early February 1942, though weak with hunger, malaria and dysentery, the aptly termed 'Battling Bastards of Bataan' had taken a heavy toll on General Homma's forces. The Japanese had advanced more than halfway down the Bataan peninsula, but they were exhausted, sick, and battered. Homma called off all ground action on February 8th and appealed to Imperial Headquarters for reinforcements. In the meantime, Japanese air and artillery strikes continued, and the New Mexicans of the 200th Coast Artillery responded in kind.

By early March, rations for the Filamericans were cut in half again. Now on less than 900 calories a day, the food was only a fourth of what was needed for active combat troops. Bataan's few remaining carabao were hunted down and butchered, and many troops resorted to eating lizards and monkeys. Finally, General Wainwright's brave 26th Cavalry horses, including his prize jumping horse, Joseph Conrad, were slaughtered and eaten. Besieged by the starving, sickened, and wounded men, Pecos Finley and the Bataan quartermasters requested that Wainwright appeal to MacArthur on Corregidor for more food and medicine. Skinny knew what the reply would be, but he did it anyway. Corregidor, though relatively well stocked with canned meats, coconut, powdered milk, rice and quinine, could not aid the Bataan defenders. MacArthur, sensing a hopeless situation on Bataan, but unwilling to acknowledge it, knew the only hope was for Corregidor to hold out as long as possible. If Corregidor had supplies to withstand a long siege, Roosevelt's promised relief force just might arrive in time to prevent disaster. If need be, Bataan would have to be sacrificed for that possibility.

The truth was that Roosevelt and General Marshall never seriously contemplated a 'relief force.' Although Australian and American ships made several brave attempts under a plan devised by American General Patrick Hurley, Japanese mastery of the air and sea lanes made any sea-borne relief impossible. Roosevelt's promises were really nothing but an orchestrated scheme to temporarily boost the spirit of the Bataan defenders and the American public.

As they welcomed a temporary respite in the ground action, Bill Porter's and Charlie Sparks' infantry units on Bataan did not know the truth. But neither were they convinced by the hollow promises and pep talks. Bill Porter's letter to his folks in New Mexico hinted at the sinking morale.

March 6, 1942
Bataan
Dearest Folks:
    I was just this minute informed that I could get a letter through to you if it reached Regimental C.P. before 1 pm. It's now 11:40 so I'll have to hurry.

It seems ages since I've heard from you, and I've worried countless nights because I know that you too are anxious about me, and I don't want you to worry. There are so many things I want to tell you and can't—experiences, stories, and what I have seen, my personal estimates, (etc., etc.) but that is impossible.

I am now a Captain and have a battalion of infantry. The going has been tough, but it will take a lot more to bust us. I received the Silver Star citation, and another, but it is still in the mill. I lost all my belongings ... . My health has been excellent; but a recent case of dengue fever laid me down for a few days. Some of the Japs seem very good, others very poor ... they have lots of guts and fight with a different outlook than we do. I am convinced that we will win this war whether the situation in the Far East becomes temporarily favorable to them or not ... several of my good friends are gone.

At first battle frightens you, no matter how many engagements you see; but after you warm up, in a few minutes all fear leaves ... and at times it is just exciting. The hardest thing is to put up with the doubt, and waiting for help—we live on rumor after rumor.

I never knew ... how much I loved you all and what you meant to me. Maybe I never really appreciated what wonderful parents you really are. This war has made me appreciate ... the little things in life—a decent smoke, a good bed, a Sunday ride ... all these things are so impossible now.

The more you see of death the more contempt you hold for it. Anything as wonderful as the human body which can think, love, work, figure and reason, and yet can be reduced to corruption in 24 hours must have within it some property such as a soul ... . The flesh is weak—it is nothing—it is the most unlasting of substances. I hold death in contempt, and yet respect it because of my most ardent desire to see you, and home once again.

Never worry about me, you must not, and I will have less on my mind, and before long I will meet you all again where we can have long days together ... . Give my love to all the folks, keep your heads up, and I'll keep mine down.

As ever,
Bill

As the situation on Bataan worsened, President Roosevelt ordered MacArthur to leave Corregidor. Fearful of the impact on morale, MacArthur stalled for time. Roosevelt gave him a few weeks. In mid-March MacArthur, wife Jean, young son Arthur, and Chinese nanny, Ah Cheu, embarked on a daring operation to run the Japanese naval blockade in PT boats. A number of MacArthur's senior staff were also ordered out with him. Under cover of night and the noise from Corregidor's big guns, MacArthur's party left in a PT boat squadron commanded by Lieutenant John Bulkeley. Before leaving, MacArthur put General Wainwright in charge. However, in a clumsy arrangement not explained to or approved by General Marshall in Washington, MacArthur intended to retain "overall command" of the Philippine forces.

After a frightful, nauseating ride and several close calls with Japanese destroyers, MacArthur's party arrived safely three days later in Mindanao in the southern Philippines.

On Mindanao at the time of MacArthur's arrival was a well known ex-Aggie, 1st Lieutenant Albert Bacon Fall Chase. A ROTC graduate, Chase had been sent to Mindanao in summer 1941 from Fort McKinley in Manila. At home in Ruidoso, Chase's mother, Alexina Fall Chase, later received touching letters from a Jesuit priest, Father Cervini. Chase had spent many evenings with the Father who described how Chase, commanding a battalion of the 73rd Regiment, 81st Division, was one of the first to engage the Japanese when they landed on Mindanao in April 1942. He received the Bronze Star for his actions before his capture and imprisonment at Davao in May 1942.

It took a day before an airworthy B-17 could get to Del Monte Field where MacArthur and family were waiting. MacArthur then flew safely to Darwin, Australia, with Japanese fighters hot on the tail of his B-17. MacArthur's wife and child, already nauseous from the long PT boat ordeal, became air sick. Arthur's condition worsened, and he was put on intravenous fluids. None of the party wanted anymore airplanes or boats, but they were still thousands of miles from their destination of Melbourne. MacArthur inquired about a train. The nearest railhead to Melbourne was at Alice Springs, a thousand miles away. After gathering themselves, MacArthur's party boarded DC-3s and flew to Alice Springs where they climbed aboard an antiquated old train. It took days to reach Melbourne, but everyone's health improved and the drama in the press created by the slow train trip was pure MacArthurese. When he finally arrived in Melbourne, MacArthur received a hero's welcome.

Back on Bataan, a newly reinforced and rested Japanese infantry was readying to attack once again. A series of coordinated air and artillery bombardments ensued in late March. This time, the barrage sent the weakened Filamericans reeling. Incendiary bombs and shells ignited the tall grass along the Bagac-Orion line where Porter and Sparks' battalions were situated. The fire and fury terrified the Filipinos. Many broke and ran. Porter, Sparks, and the other officers patiently coaxed many back to their foxholes. But as the bombardment continued, they broke again.

Following a brief lull, an all out Japanese offensive began on Good Friday, April 3rd. The offensive began with an incredible artillery barrage, the largest of the Pacific War. The barrage shook all of southern Bataan. That night, Captain Rey Gonzales of the 200th led anti-aircraft Battery F forward to cover the howitzers that were returning fire at Japanese tanks and infantrymen. The battle raged for three days before the exhausted Filamerican infantry withdrew. The New Mexicans of the 200th were ordered back. But Gonzales' failed to get the word. His three guns blazed away at the advancing Japanese. At 200th headquarters, it was feared that Battery F had been overrun by the powerful onslaught. But late on the afternoon of April 6th Gonzales appeared, leading his exhausted men. He had escaped and saved his battery.

The dazed men of the 200th now awaited orders. Ominously, the Japanese artillery began again, a prelude to a furious, powerful infantry attack.

Meanwhile, Bill Porter and Charlie Sparks tried to rally their outmanned Philippine infantrymen. On April 3rd, Sparks' unit was heavily shelled and bombed with incendiaries. But he led his men out of the foxholes and counterattacked in an attempt to outflank the advancing Japanese infantry. They fought bravely, but Sparks' men were weak. Exhausted, sick, outgunned, and without air support, they faced tanks and a fresh, well-fed enemy. It was simply too much. The defenders crumbled and retreated in chaos.

The II Corps line and 41st Division cracked. Panic ensued, and an all out rout was on. Sparks' attempted to maintain some semblance of order, but most of the dazed, shocked Filipino troops could not be stopped. They were too weak to do anything but retreat. On the I Corps side, the Japanese attack was not so powerful. But try as they might, I Corps could not come to the aid of II Corps—the mountains cut them off.

On April 7th, Major Anthony George of the 200th, Battery D, was ordered to move forward to confirm the extent of the Japanese advance on the east side. George, former All Border Conference guard on the 1936 Aggie Sun Bowl team had, during the 1935 season, snatched the ball from University of New Mexico quarterback Abie Paiz and raced 96 yards to a touchdown. He used that speed to follow his orders. George moved quickly to the front line. At 6:00 p.m., from a hidden vantage point, he radioed General Edward P. King's headquarters that the Japanese were within five miles of his battery's position a few miles up the east side road leading to the southern tip of Bataan. King asked George to determine the exact location and strength of the enemy and to stand by. An hour later, orders came to

George and the 200th. Destroy all antiaircraft equipment that couldn't be moved south or used by the infantry. Move south to form a last line of resistance near Cabcaben.

Soon the trails leading from the north to the southern tip of Bataan were disgorging thousands of bleeding, shell-shocked troops. Porter and Sparks led the remnants of their units into the hills north of Cabcaben. There was little fighting capability left. On April 8th, the 200th was designated a provisional infantry brigade and ordered to move forward again to help form the last line of defense. They were issued rifles and were instructed to fight as infantrymen. The 200th began wholesale destruction of their remaining anti-aircraft guns. Meanwhile, Pecos Finley and the quartermaster troops were blowing up ammunition dumps and sabotaging equipment at Cabcaben and Mariveles to prevent their use by the Japanese.

Colonel Carlos Romulo, the 'Voice of Freedom' whose broadcasts from Corregidor had brought comfort to the Filamerican troops during the Battle of Bataan, was ordered out by Wainwright. The Japanese had a large price on his head. Romulo crossed from Corregidor on a motor launch and went by jeep against the tide of retreating troops to the airstrip at Cabcaben. When Romulo arrived at the airstrip, an old Gruman Duck of the Bamboo Air Force awaited him. The battered plane was being hastily repaired with cannibalized parts. Loaded down with six passengers and baggage, it sputtered to a start and vibrated convulsively. Captain Roland Barnick, fighting the controls, gunned the engines and labored down the runway. The plane shuddered, barely lifted off, then dipped to within a few feet of the water. The engines on the old Duck were wide open. Swearing loudly, Barnick passed a note over his shoulder to his passengers. "Throw out all extra weight. Hurry!"

Romulo and the other five passengers threw out baggage, helmets, radio equipment, parachutes, pistols, and pieces of floorboard. The plane gradually gained altitude, passed Corregidor, and headed for Panay, more than 200 miles to the south. They would make it!

During the horrific night of April 8th, amidst the exploding dumps, the Japanese shells, and the murderous American return fire from the big guns on Corregidor, there was a Biblical-like happening. At 9:30 p.m., as if on cue from above, a powerful earthquake struck Bataan. It hardly fazed the bewildered, exhausted men. For they knew there would be no heaven sent miracles. They sensed that tomorrow, April 9th, was judgment day.

At Hospitals Nos. 1 and 2 at Cabcaben, Aggie Neil Foster was among the medical personnel, doctors, and nurses working feverishly on the massive overload of wounded and sick men. Thousands lay about, some in silent shock, some moaning in pain; all wincing as the explosions reverberated around them.

Soon word arrived from Wainwright—the nurses at the hospitals were ordered to the docks for evacuation to Corregidor. The waters between Mariveles and Corregidor were alive with swimmers and small boats full of troops seeking safety on the 'Rock.' Explosions rocked and lit up the damp night air. And from every trail and road, the beaten Bataan defenders staggered south before the powerful Japanese attack.

From Australia, MacArthur radioed orders to Wainwright on Corregidor to counterattack along the I Corps area on the west side of Bataan. Wainwright got the message and sagged as if punched in the solar plexus. Skinny knew MacArthur's orders were insanity. His troops had nothing left. Many could barely crawl out of their foxholes. Reluctantly, he passed the order to General King, his commander on Bataan. King agonized. Then after consultation with his commanders and without communicating with Wainwright, he made a momentous decision. There would be no suicidal counterattack. King had decided to surrender the Bataan forces to General Homma the next morning, April 9th. He did so to avoid the complete slaughter of some 80,000 troops and civilians. Under the circumstances it was the right decision, and a very courageous decision.

In *Beyond Courage*, Cave described the final hours of the 200th as the New Mexicans stood alone on the last ridge above Cabcaben.

> *The men on the ridge watched for dawn, and looked from their foxholes at the open field below, across which the Japanese tanks would roll at first light. They could see the enemy's campfires winking in the jungle just beyond, and could hear their laughter. They awaited the battle they knew would be their last. And they were very, very tired.*
>
> *[Winston] Shillito's platoon was positioned on the far north end. He took the end of the line, where a trail headed down into a canyon that ran to Cabcaben. The enemy waited just below. Daylight would come soon enough. He lay across the path to sleep.*
>
> *Shillito awoke suddenly. Someone had just stepped over him. He tensed, opened his eyes cautiously, and saw Major Paul Schurtz descending the trail ... . King was surrendering, Schurtz told him. At any moment a Jeep flying a white flag would pass through to try and make contact with the enemy and arrange a cease-fire. Avoid combat, King ordered, unless fired upon.*

The surrender did not go smoothly. Japanese General Kameichiro Nagano at first refused to accept King's offer to surrender Bataan, unless Corregidor was also surrendered. Nagano said King would have to talk directly with Homma's representative, since Homma's instructions were to only accept surrender if Corregidor and all other Luzon forces were included. A while later a Cadillac arrived bearing Colonel Motoo Nakayama, Homma's representative.

"You are General Wainwright?" bellowed Nakayama sarcastically. "We want to see Wainwright! We cannot accept surrender without Wainwright"

King remained cool and dignified. He tried to reason with the fuming Nakayama, explaining that Wainwright was on Corregidor and that he could surrender only the Bataan forces under his command. They argued, bluffed, and blustered. Finally, Nakayama acquiesced, but only if King surrendered unconditionally. King bartered for assurances about how the surrender and incarceration would be handled.

"Would the Japanese honor the Geneva Convention for treatment of prisoners?" King asked. "The Japanese are not barbarians," came the reply.

King was instructed to have his troops move south for assembly at Cabcaben. There, he was told, the Japanese would stage the prisoners for motor transport to Camp O'Donnell in northern Luzon. King offered the use of American trucks and gasoline that he had purposely held back from destruction for just such a use. The Japanese refused.

News of the surrender did not get to all units. Japanese bombing and shelling continued for several days. One Filamerican unit in I Corps, a battalion of the 1st Philippine Division, had not gotten the word and ambushed a Japanese unit. Bill Porter's unit also did not get the surrender order in a timely manner. They held out in the hills above Mariveles for several days, hoping for orders to counterattack. But counterattack orders did not come. They finally received word of the surrender and were forced to lay down their guns.

The Japanese were ill prepared to receive the 60,000 troops (15,000 Americans) and 20,000 civilians who surrendered on April 9th. They had anticipated maybe half that number. The original Japanese plan was to move the POWs by truck, either all the way to O'Donnell, or at least to the railhead at San Fernando, some 60 miles from Mariveles.

The surrender scene at Cabcaben and Mariveles was horrific. While some of the Japanese were merciful and professional in their actions, most were not. They repeatedly beat, strip-searched, and looted the Filipinos and Americans. They shoved wounded in front of onrushing trucks, laughing sadistically as they were run over. Prisoners were hit with sticks and rifle butts, then made to stand in the hot sun for hours without water. Periodically, a Japanese guard or officer would scream inexplicable gibberish, and throw a tantrum when their 'orders' went unobeyed. Then the prisoners would be slapped and beaten again.

At Balanga along the east road, 300 Filipino officers and men of the 1st Division who had surrendered were bound with piano wire and prodded along a jungle trail by bayonet. At a 100-foot bluff overlooking a tributary of the Pantingan River they were ordered to sit down. In groups of several dozen, they were led into the nearby jungle while the others waited and listened as their terror-stricken comrades pleaded for mercy. Then they heard the brutal warrior-like screams of the Japanese as they worked their gleaming bayonets and sabers, stabbing and beheading the Filipinos. For those who waited in agony, their turn soon came. The Japanese were exacting revenge for the post-surrender ambush by the Filipino battalion a few nights earlier.

DEATH MARCH AND CORREGIDOR

Las Cruces High graduate Winston Shillito was among the 200th men on the front line above Cabcaben when surrender came. He was captured early by a Japanese unit that was more merciful than most. In a stroke of providence, Shillito and several other New Mexicans were driven the 80 miles to Camp O'Donnell where most of the Bataan POWs were to be imprisoned.

Shillito rode part way to O'Donnell in a Japanese truck with General King. They received some rough treatment, although nothing compared to the horrors that later befell those POWs who made the Death March. Shillito and General King were denied water on the trip to O'Donnell and became very thirsty. At one of the stops, Shillito noticed a Japanese guard on the truck who was eyeing his wristwatch. He bartered his watch for a bottle of beer which was shared with King and the others.

Most of those who followed Shillito endured the infamous Bataan Death March that claimed 20,000 Filamerican lives. In actuality, the Death March was not a single event, but a series of chaotic movements by groups of POWs, prodded along by revengeful Japanese guards. Although there were exceptions—the forlorn Filamericans remembered a few acts of kindness—much of the POWs treatment was beyond sadism. It was common for no food to be issued for 48 to 72 hours, and then only a handful or two of rice. The Japanese used the lack of water to torture the weakened men. Despite the presence of artesian wells along the course of the March, most of the prisoners were not allowed a drink until the nightly rest period. Even then, some were denied water, or because of the endless water lines, were too weak to get any. Clubbings, bayonetings, beheadings, and hours in the blazing sun and dust without headcover were all part of the treatment. Then came more looting, strip-searches, bullying, and double-timing whenever a fresh guard took over a marching column. At the end of the day came unspeakable filth in the large nightly holding areas. The dysentery-infested men defecated and urinated where they stood or sat.

Filipino civilians along the way who tried to feed or give water to the POWs were beaten, bayoneted, or shot. One Filipino couple who tried to give aid to the marchers was burned at the stake as a lesson for all to see. There was a final horror for those who survived the 40- to 60-mile trek from southern Bataan to San Fernando—a five-hour train ride to Capas in tiny, oven-hot railroad boxcars that were locked shut without ventilation. Hundreds passed out and scores died. Survivors of the boxcars faced a final test, a ten-mile walk to Camp O'Donnell in the tropical sun.

John Johnson, of the 200th, Portales, remembers marching some of the way with Pecos Finley and ex-Aggie footballer, Thomas 'Louie' Long, also of Portales. They had begun during one of the earliest stages of the March. After a day or so, Finley was ordered to get in a Japanese truck. At least initially, it was Japanese policy to allow American officers to be driven to Bataan. Finley bid Johnson and Long farewell, after admonishing them—"You guys are strong. Keep going. You can make it!"

Later that day, as Johnson and Long were slogging along, they came upon Finley. The Japanese truck he was riding had broken down. The three shared a grim laugh, then trudged on together through the heat and dust. According to a first-hand account later heard by Winston Shillito at O'Donnell, Finley was approached during the March and given a cigarette by an English-speaking Japanese. To those who saw it, the Japanese obviously knew Finley. The identity of the Japanese remains a mystery, although he may have met Finley or seen him play basketball during a visit to Las Cruces in the late 1930s. Whether he was a relative of one of the established Japanese families residing in the Mesilla Valley is unknown.

A day after the first New Mexicans arrived at O'Donnell, a second convoy of trucks bearing American officers appeared at the gate. Captain Rey Gonzales was among the officers in one of the trucks, and he was happy to see his buddies. As the truck wheeled in, he yelled joyfully, "Save me a place!"

But Gonzales had made the mistake of carrying 'invasion pesos' in his pocket, probably from buying food from Filipino civilians on the way to O'Donnell. Others had Jap souvenirs or leaflets. The Japanese assumed, despite denials from the POWs, that the booty had been taken from dead Nip soldiers. The guards jerked some of the offending Americans out of line. They were beaten and trussed in the sun as an example to the other POWs. The remainder, including Gonzales, were led away in shackles and ropes. Later, the Americans in camp saw some of the guards return without the ropes. Soon after, there was gunfire. The next day, several 200th men saw the corpses of the officers in an uncovered mass grave. Gonzales was among those brutally executed on April 14, 1942.

By the end of April, virtually all of the Bataan POWs had arrived at O'Donnell. Conditions at the camp were appalling. Already sick and weak from combat and the horrors of the

Death March, the men were subjected to starvation, filthy water, malaria-ridden mosquitoes, rats, and an almost complete lack of medical attention. O'Donnell was unbelievably over-crowded. The men slept on wooden slats or floors, dressed in rags and crude homemade sandals, and went weeks without bathing. For most, the diet consisted entirely of weevil-infested rice, and precious little of that. The Americans died in droves. The Filipinos, in an adjacent encampment, died even faster.

As the POWs at O'Donnell suffered and died, Corregidor continued to hold through April and into early May 1942. But gradually, the ceaseless, brutal bombardment by Japanese bombers and artillery from nearby Bataan took its toll. Corregidor's big guns were being silenced. The water system was knocked out. Malinta Tunnel festered with dust, disease, and despair. Casualties mounted.

The account of Associated Press correspondent Clark Lee depicted the awful conditions in Malinta Tunnel.

> *The bombs didn't screech or whistle or whine. They sounded like a pile of planks being whirled around in the air by a terrific wind and driven straight down to the ground. The bombs took thirty years to hit. While they were falling they changed the dimensions of the world. The noise stripped the eagles from the colonel's shoulders and left him a little boy, naked and afraid. It drove all the intelligence from the nurse's eyes and left them vacant and staring. It wrapped a steel tourniquet of fear around your head, until your skull felt like bursting.*
>
> *Then would come the fires, and the heroism. Men and women dashing out and picking up the wounded while the bombs were still falling. They would carry the dead and the wounded to the hospital tunnel. You would hear the cars ... the urgency of their horns, blowing all the way down the hill from Topside and then up the slope from Bottomside ... MPs would make the cars slow down ... and they would stop at the hospital tunnel and blood would be dripping ... then the stretcher bearers would gently lift out the bloody remnants of what had been an American soldier or a Filipino worker .... They would lift out the handsome captain whose legs were bloody stumps ... they would lift out the eighteen-year-old American boy who would never again remember his name, but would just look at you blankly when your spoke to him.*

... In the tunnel, though safe from exploding shells and bombs, men were under great emotional stress. The thick walls ... formed a haven, but they were also a prison. The constant heat ... the huge black flies and vermin, and the worsening smells of the hospital and the tightly packed unwashed bodies were the parameters of a world without sunlight or a cooling ocean breeze or a moment of privacy.

On April 17th, Wainwright ordered a seaplane to bring in medicines and take out civilian women, nurses, and some of the older American officers that he knew could stand no more strain. He got word on April 29th that two planes would be sent, but there would be room for no more than fifty passengers. MacArthur sent Wainwright a list of personnel he needed, including several Japanese-speaking officers and cryptographers. Skinny chose the rest—the civilian women and children, a few key pilots, and six elderly officers. It left room for only thirty of the 150 nurses.

At 11:00 p.m. on April 29th, the seaplanes arrived in clear skies south of Corregidor. Two small naval vessels revved their engines to mask the noise of the incoming planes. They had removed the engine mufflers and the racket reverberated across to Bataan. The Japanese did not detect the seaplanes. Wainwright led a convoy of battered vehicles from Malinta Tunnel down to the south docks at Bottomside. The docks were in splinters from the shelling and bombing. As the evacuees boarded the boats that would take them to the seaplanes, Skinny shook hands with the men and hugged the nurses. Nurse Juanita Redmond kissed him on the cheek and said a tearful thank you. Wainwright stayed on the dock staring out at the water until the two planes lifted off.

The vicious bombardment of Corregidor continued, unrelenting, constant. Now the water system was working only periodically, and much of the communication system to the defenders outside the tunnel was wasted, irreparable. On May 1st, Wainwright ordered his radiomen to transmit names and serial numbers of all known American servicemen in the Philippines to the U.S. He ordered his finance officer to prepare eighteen trunks of records for shipment on a submarine (the last) which would reach Corregidor in a few days. These records proved invaluable when the war ended more than three years later.

Late on May 5, 1942, after an incredibly fierce bombardment, there was a deathly silence. The lull was what Wainwright had long feared. With the intuition of an old cavalryman, Skinny sensed what was coming. Soon noise detectors picked up the sounds of landing barges full of Japanese troops approaching Corregidor from Bataan. Then, small arms fire reverberated. A last valiant stand by the Marines and other Filamerican troops on Corregidor killed hundreds of the Japanese before they could leave the barges. The slaughter was savage, but it did not stop them. In a few hours, hundreds of 'ant men' and tanks were seen moving up the road toward Malinta Tunnel. The vision of tanks firing into the tunnel filled with wounded men and nurses was unthinkable to Wainwright. He would have to act.

In his book *Hero of Bataan*, Duane Shultz wrote of Wainwright:

> *When his big chance came, on Bataan and on Corregidor, he had to fight a static war, a war of strong lines of defence. It was not the war he had trained for, the war of dashing and daring raids, of canteen clicking on leather and a strong horse beneath him. It was a war in a jungle where a man could barely walk, a war of foxholes and trenches. War in a concrete tunnel, dank and dark, that shook from bombs and shells. There were no cavalry charges for Wainwright. How he must have hated that.*

It was against every instinct in Wainwright's being to surrender. He felt humiliated, and would worry incessantly through his years in Japanese prison camps whether he would be court martialed if he lived to return to the U.S. But Skinny knew what he must do and he faced up to it. A party was sent out with white flags toward the approaching enemy troops. Arrangements were made for Wainwright to go to Bataan to meet with the Japanese.

There, despite Wainwright's protests that MacArthur was still in charge of the Philippine forces (which he was not), the Japanese insisted that he surrender the entire Philippines. Wainwright at first refused, but General Homma persisted. Finally, with no real choice, Skinny accepted the inevitable. A complete Filamerican surrender was official on May 6, 1942. Wainwright was taken to Manila and forced to conduct radio broadcasts announcing the surrender. The Japanese ordered him to select American officers to go to the other Philippine islands to spread the word personally. Otherwise, it was feared the Filamericans would continue fighting. If that happened, Wainwright was told that the Japanese would take reprisals against the POWs.

Many of the newly captured Americans from Corregidor were paraded through Manila in a show designed to humiliate them before the Filipinos. The Japanese propaganda machine had declared the Philippines, and other captured Asian and Pacific lands, as the new 'Greater East Asia Co-Prosperity Sphere.' The scheme was to convince the natives to unite as brown-skinned brothers and sisters against the white-skinned colonial Americans and Europeans. The Americans were made to grovel before the conquering and superior Japanese. Soon, the new POW's streamed into O'Donnell and the other camps on Luzon.

At O'Donnell, the Corregidor POW's were shocked at the filthy, emaciated skeletons they saw when they arrived. By the end of May 1942, more than 1500 POWs had died at

O'Donnell, including some 100 New Mexicans. Their number included ex-Aggies Private George Huston (Lovington, '30?) and Private First Class Byron Beal (Elida, '39), both of the 200th. In May, Lieutenant L.W. Rogers (Santa Fe, '40) passed away. Dysentery, malaria, beri beri, and diphtheria, were rampant at O'Donnell. These diseases could and did kill even the strongest in a matter of a few days. In late May 1942, the Japanese readied to move most of the POWs to a new camp at Cabanatuan thirty miles to the east. Bill Porter and Pecos Finley lay deathly sick, racked with dysentery and malaria. Their New Mexico compadres gave them little chance for survival.

At Cabanatuan conditions were only a little better than at O'Donnell, and the weakened men continued to die. Although exact circumstances are not know, it was probably just after arriving at Cabanatuan that Pecos Finley died. At the time, those in Las Cruces had no knowledge of Finley's death or any inkling of the Death March and the Japanese brutality in the POW camps. In fact, Finley's mother, Ada Ralston of Causey, was reported to have heard Pecos on a Japanese radio broadcast just after the fall of Bataan.

At the time of Finley's death, Bill Porter lay in 'Zero Ward,' a section of the Cabanatuan POW camp reserved for those beyond help. Winston Shillito had seen Porter with his own eyes and was sure he was near death. Delirious and tormented with Dysentery and malaria, he would roll off his slatted bed into the warmth of the morning sun. His combrades would pick him up and bring him inside. Somehow, miraculously, Bill Porter gained strength and survived. He was proving to be one tough cowboy.

But others, including many ex-Aggies, died in droves. Captain Charles Sparks died on June 21, 1942. Sergeant Lew Calkins (Albuquerque, '27), 200th, succumed on July 13th. Corporal William Love (Deming, '40), 200th, passed away on August 24th. Sergeant John Flowers (Lake Arthur, '36), 200th, died on September 11th. With hundreds of others, the dead Aggies were buried by their fellow prisoners in shallow, water-logged graves. Many of the corpses were dug up and eaten by packs of marauding, starving dogs.

Private First Class Louie Long, strapping blonde ex-Aggie footballer, was just the type of 'large' American the Japanese guards at Cabanatuan like to bait and abuse. On August 28, 1942, Long did something that displeased a guard. Approached by a jabbering Japanese officer and seeing that he was going to be beaten again, Long showed his contempt by spitting in the officer's face. He was promptly shot in front of his fellow POWs.

Still hanging to a thread of life at Cabanatuan was another Aggie, 1st Lieutenant William Trogstad of Las Vegas. But after a long bout of malaria and dysentery, he succumed on November 7, 1942. Meanwhile, his wife Martha languished under harsh conditions at Los Banos prison south of Manila, unaware of her husband's death.

Several hundred miles south of Manila on the big island of Mindanao, was the Davao POW camp. Aggies at Davao included 1st Lieutenants Robert Remondini (Deming, '39), 200th, and the aforementioned Albert Chase of Three Rivers. Remondini had apparently been transferred on work detail from the POW camp at Cabanatuan. After leading heroic fights on Mindanao and Cebu Island, Chase's unit of the 73rd Infantry unit had been captured during the Philippine-wide surrender ordered by General Wainwright in May 1942.

As the Japanese war effort took its toll on manpower in the home islands, the American POWs were asked to 'volunteer' as specialists for work in Japanese industry. Given the horrific conditions in the camps, many did. Thus, began the Japanese program of shipping POWs out of the Philippines in unmarked ships. Easy targets for American submarines and planes, these stinking cargo vessels were to become infamous as the 'Hell Ships.'

On October 8, 1942, the *Tottori Maru* left Manila Bay with 1,200 Americans, many of whom where New Mexicans, including Winston Shillito and Anthony George.

The Japanese skipper of the *Tottori* deftly evaded several American torpedoes at the start of the voyage and was actually applauded by the Americans, to which the skipper grinned and tipped his cap. But that's where the fun ended. Crammed into a dark, filthy hold, the men became deranged and desperately sick. Those who died were flung overboard. The voyage took weeks and the weather changed from tropical to freezing. After landing in Korea and Manchuria, the *Tottori* made for Moji, Japan. Shillito, George, and their 200th compadres on board could thank their lucky stars again. They had survived, and compared to what happened on later 'Hell Ship' voyages, they were indeed blessed.

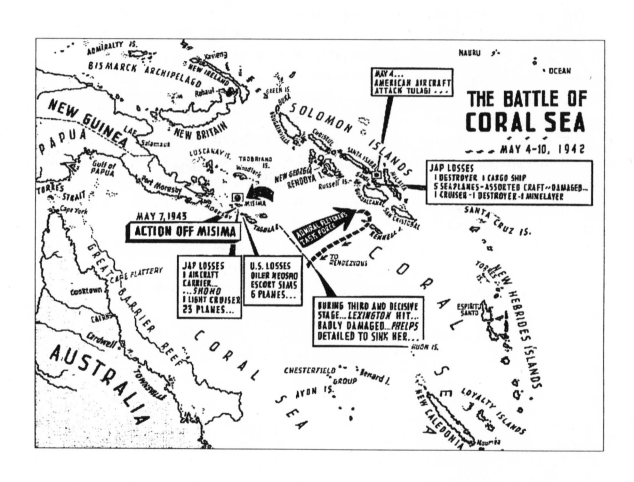

CORAL SEA AND GUADALCANAL

In April 1942, the Joint Chiefs had given MacArthur command of the 'Southwest Pacific Area' from his new headquarters in Australia. The Navy's Admiral Chester Nimitz was given command of the 'South Pacific Area.' MacArthur's territory included Australia, New Guinea, much of the Solomons (but not Guadalcanal), and the other islands to the northwest leading to the Philippines. American troops and supplies began arriving in Australia. A massive jungle and amphibious landing training complex was established on New Caledonia, some 1,000 miles off the Australian coast in the New Hebrides. An Army Air Corps base was established at Espiritu Santo several hundred miles south of Guadalcanal. The 1st Marine Division was sent to Wellington, New Zealand. Though the American fighting men were not combat tested, the build up in the Pacific was finally on, and it was formidable.

MacArthur's overriding assignment was a tough one—taking back the Bismarck Archipelago and the huge Japanese base at Rabaul on New Britain. Besides Rabaul with its 100,000 troops, airfields and large harbor, the Japanese were entrenched in New Ireland, on Slamaua and Lae in New Guinea, on Bougainville Island, and several smaller islands in the western Solomons.

With the American presence at Espiritu Santo, the Japanese recognized the need to have an air base in the eastern Solomons. In early May 1942, the Japanese landed at Tulagai on Florida Island near Guadalcanal. American intelligence feared, correctly, that the next step would be an airfield on Guadalcanal. While they were landing at Tulagai, the Japanese readied a massive sea and air force to attack and occupy Port Moresby, New Guinea, on the Coral Sea.

Enter the American fleet, led by the carriers *Yorktown* and *Lexington*, the latter with Marine Lieutenant Henry Gustafson aboard. Gustafson had been on constant patrol on the *Lexington* since his narrow escape at Pearl Harbor in December 1941. On May 4th, naval aircraft from the *Lexington* and the *Yorktown*, plastered the Japanese ships and sea planes that were supporting the landing at Tulagai. The task force then headed northwest where American scout planes had spotted the Japanese attack force moving toward Port Moresby.

The stage was set for the first major sea battle of the Pacific War. It was exclusively fought with naval aircraft at long range. The battle continued for two days. On board the *Lexington*, Gustafson remembered: "I had a station aft of the stack. I had a great view, but no protection from the Japanese fighters and dive bombers that attacked us." A group of Japanese torpedo bombers loosed their deadly fish from both port and starboard. Two struck home. As the *Lexington* shuddered, she was hit again by a 1,000-pound bomb that struck the flight deck near the first torpedo hit, then by a 500-pounder. Explosions and fires raged. Brave crews worked feverishly to control the damage, and for awhile they gained an upper hand. Then a tremendous internal explosion shook the carrier and the fires began anew.

Late in the afternoon of May 8th, Captain Frederick Sherman got on the bullhorn. "All hands abandon ship," he ordered. Nearly 3,000 crewman swarmed over the side using cargo nets and ropes. Some jumped. Gustafson went down on a rope and swam away from the fiercely burning ship. He and a buddy finally clambered aboard a 12-man life raft and began picking up other survivors. American cruisers and destroyers converged on the area and picked up Gustafson and the other survivors. Late in the evening, two American destroyers finished off the stricken *Lexington* with torpedoes. Many tears were shed as the men saw their gallant ship slip beneath the waves. But amazingly, more than 90 percent of the *Lexington* crew had been saved.

When the Battle of the Coral Sea was over, the Japanese had lost one carrier sunk, two others crippled, and several lesser ships damaged and sunk. The Japanese also lost more than 100 planes and 5,000 men. U.S. losses were heavy—543 lives, 66 planes, and three ships, including the mighty *Lexington*. In reality, the battle was a draw—except for one thing. Japanese plans for attacking and occupying Port Moresby had been thwarted. The Japanese dream of using Port Moresby as a base for a drive on Australia was never to be. The long string of Japanese offensive successes had been stopped.

Gustafson was shipped back to San Diego on June 2, 1942 after a brief stay on the Tonga Islands. He called his fiancé, Caroline Kiser of Clayton, from San Diego. Understandably, Caroline was curious and wanted to know why Henry was back. Under orders not to speak of the *Lexington*, Gustafson stammered and made up a story about coming back to "get some uniforms." Caroline didn't buy that and went to State College to see Colonel Chilton. As usual, Chilton gave sage advice. "Why don't you go to San Diego and see for yourself?" he suggested. A few days later in the company of Gustafson's father, mother, and brother, she walked in on a surprised Gustafson. Henry and Caroline were married in Clayton on June 21, 1942.

On May 10, 1942, as the Battle of the Coral Sea was joined, ex-Aggie halfback Mert Gillis (Marshall, TX, '38) and a large contingent of the 1st Marine Division left the east coast bound for New Zealand. Gillis, a junior college transfer, had not gone through ROTC at NM A&M. But he wanted to be a Marine and had volunteered and entered WW II as a private. Upon arrival in Wellington, Gillis and his Marine compadres received royal treatment from the grateful Kiwis. But it wasn't all fun. The Marines also worked hard practicing amphibious landings, combat maneuvers, and gunnery. They did calisthenics and ran almost every day. But at the end of the day, there was plenty of excellent beer and gracious hospitality from the natives.

By early summer 1942, the men of the 1st Marine Division had their orders—*take Guadalcanal at all costs*! After staging and loading their ships, the Division left for the invasion of Guadalcanal in early August. It would be the first U.S. offensive land action of the Pacific War. The Marines were charged with capturing the Japanese airfield and securing Guadalcanal as the southern anchor for the retaking of the western Solomons; and, eventually, the grand prize—Rabaul on New Britain. Many gave the Marines little chance.

The Marines landed at Guadalcanal on August 7th to surprisingly light resistance. 'landing luck' they called it. The Japanese onshore were shocked by the sheer bravado of the action, and the few troops at the airstrip made for the jungle upon experiencing the pre-invasion bombardment. But the enemy soon regrouped, and the Marines came under fierce counter-attack by the enraged Japanese. The next few months would witness some of the most vicious, dirty fighting imaginable. And all around the Marines, there raged a series of bloody sea and air battles. From their fortress at Rabaul, 800 miles to the northwest, Japanese soldiers, airmen and sailors streamed into Guadalcanal. They now knew the importance of the island and they were dogged in their attempts to drive the Marines off. Guadalcanal's Henderson Field became the home of the 'Cactus Air Force,' a wild concoction of Marine and Army flyers who, against all odds, defended Guadalcanal with a vengence.

One of the critical sea battles of the Guadalcanal campaign occurred on the moonless evening of August 8, 1942, just after the landing on Guadalcanal. Under Admiral Gun'ichi Mikawa, the Japanese dispatched a powerful naval force with simple orders: "Destroy the American landing and cargo vessels at Tulagi and Guadalcanal." Mikawa was after the transports at the beachheads, but he knew there would be American cruisers and carriers supporting the landing force. He would use stealth, surprise, and darkness in his well-planned attack.

Among the American ships taking up night screening positions near Savo Island just off Guadalcanal on August 8, 1942 was the cruiser *Astoria*. On board was Aggie Seaman 2nd Class Charles Leon Billups (Alamogordo, '41). His brother Ben Billups was then a Captain with the 120th Combat Engineers, a New Mexico National Guard unit that saw action with the 45th Division throughout Africa, Italy, France, and Germany. Another Billups brother, Eugene served with the Signal Service of the U.S. Air Corps in India.

At 1:50 a.m. on August 9th, a lookout on the *Astoria* saw a glow to the south, then a ship opening fire at a long distance. He rang the general alarm, and Billups and his mates went to full battle stations. But it was too late. Japanese searchlights illuminated the *Astoria* and her sister ship, the *Vincennes*. A firestorm of enemy shells engulfed the two ships, and a third American ship, the *Quincy*. The *Astoria* was the first to return fire. But immediately, she and the other ships received devastating hits. The *Quincy*, trapped between two Japanese cruisers, became a burning inferno. Soon she radioed, "We're going down between them—give 'em hell!"

The *Astoria* fired the last American salvo at 2:15 a.m., only to receive a massive barrage of return fire. Now there was no steering control, and soon, no engine power. Just as the battle seemed won, the Japanese mysteriously withdrew without pressing the attack further. Later they learned that the navigation charts in the flagship *Chokai* had been destroyed by American shells and that Admiral Mikawa had heard American broadcasts readying for an air attack at dawn. Thus, Mikawa reasoned that his force should withdraw while it was ahead.

As the Japanese broke off the attack, the *Astoria* drifted helplessly. The wounded were gathered on deck while the able bodied fought to put out the fires and save the ship. It was a vain effort, for the *Astoria* was severely damaged. She sunk at noon on August 9th.

Charles Billups was among those brave seamen killed on the *Astoria* during the Battle of Savo Island. He was buried at sea on August 9, 1942—the first Aggie to die in naval combat during the Pacific War.

Over the coming months, Mert Gillis and the valiant Marines on Guadalcanal withstood all that the Japanese and nature could throw at them. They endured daily bombings, nightly shellings by Japanese ships, landings by Japanese reinforcements, maniacal drunken banzai charges, malarial mosquitoes, leeches, stifling heat, alligators, snakes, and meager rations. But in the end, they held, though at times, just barely. On September 13-14, 1942, the Marines under Lieutenant Colonel Lewis 'Chesty' Puller fought off a determined charge of Japanese infantrymen and artillery at Bloody Nose Ridge overlooking Henderson Field. In a bitter, desperate battle, the Japanese were repulsed with more than 600 killed. Although Marine casualties were also high, the battle proved to be the turning point of Guadalcanal. The island fell securely into American hands in November 1942. The victorious Guadalcanal campaign, led by Marine and Naval forces under Admirals Nimitz and Halsey, had set the foundation for MacArthur's forces to attack the other Solomon Islands to the west. And Guadalcanal's Henderson Field became a critical air base for devastating attacks against Japanese shipping and land forces throughout the Solomons.

MORE AGGIES ANSWER THE CALL

As the POWs suffered in the Japanese camps through the summer and fall of 1942, New Mexico A&M was still a functioning college, but just barely. Only 800 students were enrolled as the fall semester began in 1942. Among the freshmen was 17-year old engineering student Jim Meadows (Elida, '50). One fall morning, Meadows and his hometown friend Bill Sturman (Elida, '48) were sitting under a tree near Hadley Hall, commiserating about an engineering test. The truth was that something else was bothering them. They were young, many of their friends had gone to war, and they were stuck in college playing with slide rules and arcane equations. They talked a while and convinced one another that they were men of action.

Meadows said to Sturman, "Let's quit school and join the Navy." After a discussion, that is exactly what they did. Leaving their books under that tree by Hadley Hall, they walked to Highway 85 and hitchhiked to El Paso. There they signed up for the Navy and were accepted, contingent on passing a physical in Santa Fe. Late that afternoon they returned to campus where they found their hated engineering books undisturbed, still under the tree by Hadley Hall.

Meadows passed his physical but Sturman didn't because of color blindness. Sturman did pass a short time later. Meadows, after getting his mother to sign the papers for under-age enlistment, left for San Diego for basic training. Following basic he went to aerial torpedomen school and was assigned to the new 'Jeep carrier' *Breton* at Bremerton, Washington. The *Breton* took on armaments and planes and had a shake-down cuirse of several months off California before leaving for the southwest Pacific in January 1943. Over the next year and a half, Meadows and the *Breton* made several runs back and forth to the U.S. ferrying planes to the New Hebrides in support of the Allied build up.

Like Meadows, Sturman saw duty on a 'Jeep carrier,' the *Copohee*. And, like Meadow's Breton, the *Copohee* spent much of the war ferrying planes to the South Pacific. Sturman and Meadows never crossed paths in the Pacific, but one day after returning to port in San Francisco they ran into one another while boarding the 'A Train.' A shoving match had broken out in the long line of troops waiting at the depot and Meadows ran over to help restore order. Standing there in the middle of the ruckus was Bill Sturman.

About the time Meadows and Sturman enlisted in the Navy in fall 1942, 1st Lieutenant Tom Esterbrook was completing training at Fort Benning, Georgia, and Fort Bragg, North Carolina. At Fort Benning, he ran into an old friend—fellow Aggie athlete Lieutenant Lem Pratt* (Las Cruces, '37). Pratt, one of the best athletes in Aggie history, had quarterbacked the 1936 Sun Bowl team that also featured cousins Hooky Apodaca (Mesilla, '36) and Lauro Apodaca (La Mesa, '37), Walt Nations, and Anthony George.

In October 1942, Esterbrook's unit, the 503rd Parachute Infantry Regiment, was ordered to the Pacific. The 503rd was loaded on a troop train and traveled westward across the continent toward San Francisco. At first, it was fun. But by the third day, the normally active men grew antsy. The trip seemed endless. The men gambled, read, griped, and finally, stared blankly at the passing scenery. When the train stopped in Elko, Nevada, the soldiers saw something irresistible—a liquor store just across the tracks. Luck was with them. Several passersby were cajoled to run back and forth to the store with hundreds of dollars to buy 'libations.' For hours, as the train crossed the foreboding desert of northern Nevada, the party raged. The noise was ignored for a long while, but finally the Regiment's officers came through the cars searching for bottles. Astonishingly, none were found, though some of the officers reported back to their car with crooked smiles that emanated a not so subtle whiskey order. Those in New Mexico who heard the story and know Tom Esterbrook are sure he was one of those grinning officers.

The 503rd made San Francisco and shipped out on October 19, 1942, for Australia on the converted Dutch freighter, *Poelau Laut*. The ship went to Balboa in the Panama Canal Zone to pick up the 501st Parachute Infantry Battalion, which was being added to the regiment. The 503rd was now at full strength—more than 1900. For the next month, the overcrowded, stiflingly hot *Poelau Laut* chugged across the vast Pacific at 12 knots. Forty-two days of monotony, interspersed with drill, instruction, and calisthenics finally ended when the ship docked at Cairns, North Queensland, Australia, on December 2, 1942. The 503rd was on firm ground again and breathing fresh air. Then they spotted the waving Australian women. "Was this heaven or what?" asked the grateful soldiers.

---

* At Fort Benning, Pratt was training with the 368th Combat Team assigned to the 1st Armored Division. He later shipped out to Italy for the duration of the war. While in Rome in 1944, Pratt met up with another friend—ex-Aggie footballer and Doña Ana County Road Superintendent, Pat McClernon (Las Cruces, '32) of the 120th Combat Engineers. The 120th was a New Mexico National Guard unit attached to the 45th Infantry Division, the same division that had famous New Mexico cartoonist Bill Mauldin. McClernon was overseeing repairs to the Rome water system, including a special assignment to repair damage to the ancient Roman aqueduct that was being blown up by German saboteurs using floating rafts loaded with dynamite.

As Esterbrook came across the Pacific, 1st Lieutenant Jack Lee had been busy terrorizing the Japanese in the Solomons. Lee, a champion Golden Gloves boxer, had roomed with Aggie Carl Freeman during his senior year at NM A&M. Freeman, who was at that time in training with the 96th Infantry Division on the West Coast, was still having nosebleeds from his previous duty as Lee's sparing partner.

By spring 1942, Jack Lee had already seen combat at the Battle of Midway with the 11th Heavy Bombardment Group, 431st Bomb Squadron, 13th Air Force. He then went to New Hebrides with some of the first army flyers in the South Pacific. By summer 1942, the 431st was flying B-17s out of a crude, secret airstrip on Espiritu Santo—both during and before the invasion of Guadalcanal. Later, after the Marines captured and made it operational in early fall 1942, Lee's squadron occasionally flew from Guadalcanal's Henderson Field with the famous 'Cactus Air Force.'

Incredibly aggressive and resourceful, these early aviators were pure poison to the Japanese. Lee served as co-pilot to Major James V. Edmundson, one of the hottest bomber pilots and air commanders in the South Pacific. Edmundson had distinguished himself at Pearl Harbor and Midway before taking over the 431st. In the Solomons, Lee and Edmundson flew many B-17 missions together bombing and strafing Japanese ships and installations on nearby islands. Their trademark was a high-speed 'wing-wagging' celebratory buzz of cheering U.S. Marines on the beaches after a successful encounter with a Japanese ship or anti-aircraft battery. In one action, Edmundson and Lee actually engaged several Jap Zeros in a dogfight and won.

By fall 1942, Lee's squadron was hitting Japanese installations on other Solomon Islands—New Georgia and Bougainville. Such missions were dangerous because the enemy airfields were filled with lightning-quick Zeros and anti-aircraft batteries. On November 18, 1942, Lee was co-pilot to Major Al Stewart on the lead B-17 that carried Colonel LaVerne Saunders, commander of an eighteen-plane bombing force attacking Bougainville. The force was jumped by twenty Zeros. The Zeros focused on the lead plane, knowing that it was key to the success of the American mission. They made coordinated strafing runs at the big B-17, and on the last one Major Stewart was killed outright by a bullet through the heart. Co-pilot Lee was hit in the ankle.

With the left engine knocked out and a wing on fire, Colonel Saunders, ex-West Point football star, jumped into the pilot's seat. He and Lee coaxed the B-17 to an emergency landing on the water near a small islet off southern Bougainville. The crew deployed rubber rafts. As Lee was being pulled out of the co-pilot's seat, a bullet from a strafing Zero tore through his stomach. The crew lifted Lee, now bleeding uncontrollably, into a raft just as the B-17 sunk. By the time they reached shore, Lieutenant Jack Lee was dead. On the beach, Saunders and the crew held a service and buried Lee under the sand to prevent detection by the Japanese who were sure to come searching. A few hours later, natives approached the survivors. The natives were under the command of the intrepid Australian coast watchers on

Bougainville who had learned of the encounter. Saunders and the others were soon in safe hands, and eventually, returned to American lines in the New Hebrides. Lee's body was never recovered.

Colonel Saunders wrote of Lee, "No more brave and gallant officer ever carried the fight to the enemy." His longtime combat buddy, Major Edmundson, wrote, "I hope that when my turn comes, I will be able to meet it like Jack did, without flinching." Edmundson and Saunders saw to it that Lee was posthumously awarded the Silver Star and the Air Medal. Like Las Cruces, Alamogordo had lost a favorite son.

Besides the 13th Air Force and the navy flyers, the Solomons-New Guinea area was the stage for the fearsome 5th Air Force of General George Kenney. Kenney encouraged his pilots to be innovative and 'hell bent.' He had the hot new P-38s, an aircraft that finally gave the Americans a match for the speed and maneuverability of the Zero. Kenney had his bombers, mostly low flying B-25s, modified to carry up to ten 50-caliber machine guns. The guns provided awesome firepower and gave enemy anti-aircraft gunners nightmares. The 5th's young pilots were taught to fly in packs, both for safety in warding off Zeros and for the shock value it had on Japanese ground forces. They developed deadly new techniques like 'skip bombing' where 500-pound bombs were dropped at 200 feet above the water while flying at 200 mph. The technique proved devastating on Japanese shipping—many times more effective than torpedo bombing or bombing from high altitude. MacArthur loved Kenney, calling him "my buccaneer." Tokyo radio labeled him "The Beast" and his pilots a "gang of gangsters."

Aggie Billy Drew Hunter (Silver City, '41) joined the 5th as a bombardier in 1942. He survived dozens of dangerous missions, but was killed when his plane was shot down over the Solomons in August 1943. He was posthumously awarded the Distinguished Flying Cross.

At the time of Lee and Hunter's deaths, there was a large group of Aggie airmen in action all over the Pacific, and many met the same fate. One was Lieutenant Leo M. Eminger who earlier had the misfortune to land in a B-17 at Hickam Field during the December 7th attack on Pearl Harbor. He was lost in air action of unknown circumstances over the Solomons in October 1942. Eminger received the Distinguished Flying Cross and the Purple Heart. Other Aggie airmen included Marine Lieutenants Ralph Ortiz (Santa Fe, '42) and Lisle Foord (Las Vegas, '42). Ortiz was killed in December 1943 in action of the Ellice Islands and was posthumously awarded the Navy Cross. Foord died over Vella Lavella Island in the Solomons in August 1944. Army Lieutenant James Wilkerson (Quay, '41) was killed in air training in Hawaii, in June 1943. Ex-Aggie footballer Lieutenant (j.g.) Joe Bloch (Breckenridge, PA, '41) was a Navy flyer killed over the Solomons in December 1943. Army Lieutenant Paul McLaughlin (Hatch, '41) was a navigator with the 7th Army Air Force who fought at Tarawa before being killed over the Central Pacific in January 1944. Staff Sergeant Charles McGinley

(Monahans, TX, '41) died in air combat over New Ireland in April 1944 after flying 31 missions with the Army Air Corps. Army Lieutenants W.J. Spence (El Paso, '41) and James S. Quesenberry (Las Cruces, '40) were both killed in air action over the Pacific in May 1944. Lieutenant Henry Provencio (??, ??) died over the Pacific in December 1944

As the air war blazed over the Pacific in late 1942, 1st Lieutenant Morris Wood arrived in the Southwest Pacific with the 43rd Infantry Division. Soon, other Aggies appeared with MacArthur's army—Captain Jim Baird (Alamogordo, '34), Captain Otis Horton (Des Moines, '41), 1st Lieutenant John H. 'Jack' Campbell (Las Cruces, '41), 1st Lieutenant Baylus Cade (Las Cruces, '41), and Captain Mansil Scrivner (Tatum, '38). All were with the 25th Infantry Regiment of the 93rd Division except Cade, who was with the 25th Division and Campbell who was with the Americal Division. Each had previously received ROTC commissions at NM A&M. Another Aggie ROTC graduate arriving at Guadalcanal was Captain Mark Radoslovich (Clayton, '41). He was originally with the 93rd Infantry Division, which was all black except for a cadre of white officers. Upon arriving in the Solomons, Radoslovich was transferred to the 43rd Division.

The highest-ranking Aggie in the Solomons was none other than President-in-Absentia, Colonel Hugh M. Milton, II. Originally from Kentucky, Milton taught mechanical engineering at Texas A&M before coming to NM A&M as a professor in 1924. His wife, Lola Orene Wilson Milton of Bryan, Texas, as an accomplished dancer who became a dance instructor at the College. When she died unexpectedly in 1929, Hugh was deeply saddened. But he threw himself into his work and was rewarded in 1933 when he was named Dean of Engineering. Also in 1933, he married Josephine 'Jo' Mae Baldwin of Corona, California. Jo, who was fourteen years younger than Hugh, came to NM A&M as a student and fell in love. She would later bear two sons—Hugh, III in 1934 and John in 1940.

In 1938, Hugh Milton took over as President of NM A&M amidst the political turmoil of the Depression and the reign of flamboyant head of the Board of Regents, Dan Williams. Milton led the College through several crises, one involving charges by Dean of Men George F. Mott that Williams had been acting as *de facto* President under the guidance of Governor John Miles. When accreditation was threatened by Mott's charges, Williams resigned from the Board of Regents in 1940. Milton appeared before the State Legislature and the North Central Association and was successful in countering the charges and reinstating the College's good name.

Throughout the late '30s and early '40s, Milton crisscrossed the state for speaking engagements at civic affairs, high school graduations, and other public meetings. A student of history and current affairs, he was a master orator with a distinct patriotic flourish. Milton maintained a commission as a Lieutenant Colonel in the Army Reserve, Chemical Corps. He became involved in the planning and application of explosives and new weapons such as napalm—a wicked substance that would be used with devastating effect in bombs and

51

flamethrowers throughout the Pacific War. When not on summer assignment with the Chemical Corps, Milton often led the Aggie ROTC cadets to summer camps in New Mexico, Texas, and Oklahoma.

On September 4, 1941, Milton was called to active duty with the Army. Jo and the boys were then left to "sweat it out" at home on campus during Hugh's long service during the Pacific War. After staging in Australia in 1943, Milton arrived in the Solomons as G-4 in the XIV Corps, U.S. Army. As the expression goes, Milton and the other Aggie soldiers were soon "up to their asses in alligators" at new Georgia, New Britain, and Bougainville.

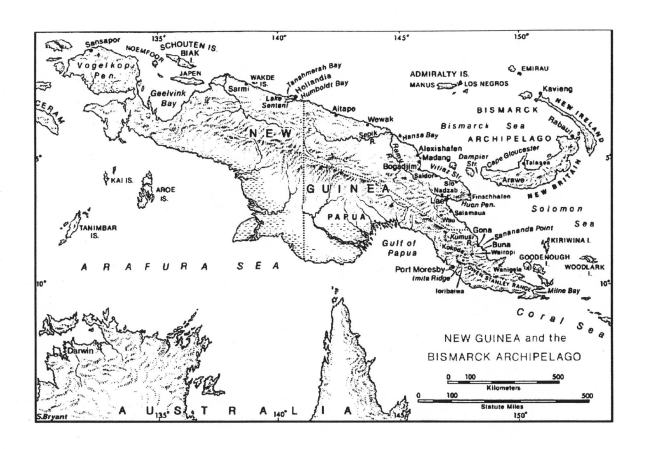

NEW GUINEA and the BISMARCK ARCHIPELAGO

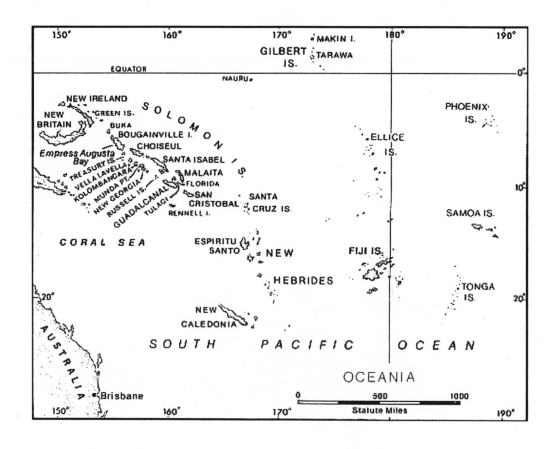

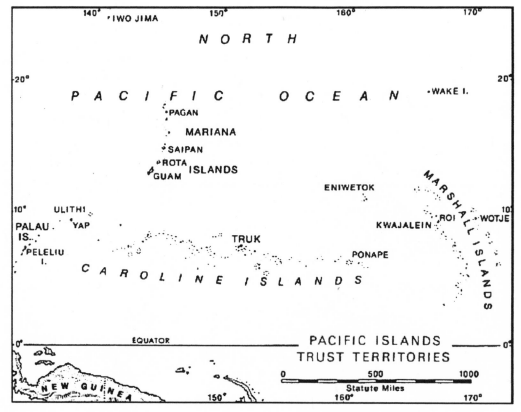

UP THE LADDER

'Pucker' Wood's 43rd Infantry Division was a National Guard unit comprised mostly of New Englanders. The Southwest Pacific couldn't have been more foreign to anyone, except possibly Eskimos. With Guadalcanal secured by the 1st Marine Division in late 1942, Wood's regiment relieved the Marines and took up garrison duty, soon after which, Radoslovich's 93rd Division arrived. In June 1943, a regiment of the 43rd Division was ordered to attack another of the Solomon Islands, New Georgia, 200 miles west of Guadalcanal.

Helping to cover the New Georgia attack was Navy Lieutenant (j.g.) Jack Durio. In summer 1941, Durio 'graduated' from 'Jett's Air Force' at NM A&M at age 20. Durio left for Navy pilot training, first at Long Beach, CA, and then at Corpus Christi, TX. He was joined in flight training by his friend and fellow Aggie Joe Resley (Las Cruces, '41). Navy Lieutenant Resley was later killed in a military plane crash at Mount Tamalpais near San Francisco on November 30, 1944.

When Durio arrived in the South Pacific after getting his Navy wings, he was soon flying dive bombing missions in support of the 43rd's attempts to take the airstrip at Munda. The Japanese had cleverly disguised the construction of the airstrip by stringing camouflage on wires between coconut palms. When their intent was finally discovered by American intelligence, the capture of the airstrip became imperative. But there were now 10,000 Japanese troops on the island, and they were tough, hardened soldiers.

The New Georgia campaign proved a brutal experience for U.S. forces, in many ways worse than Guadalcanal. The veteran Japanese jungle fighters and the horrible, marshy terrain slowed the 43rd to a crawl. The Japanese were like jungle animals, totally at home in the swamps, vines, and bushes. They sniped from trees and popped out of hidden foxholes after the Americans had passed by. They used terrifying infiltration tactics at night. Crawling for hours on their bellies, slithering into American foxholes, slitting the throats of many of the

43rd's green sentries. Several of the Japanese spoke perfect English. They were adept at luring in the green Americans by groaning and begging for medical aid as if they were wounded comrades. ... "Hey buddy. Give me a hand will ya? I'm hit bad." At other times they taunted individual American troops whose names they somehow knew ... "Joe, you chickenshit GI. Come out and die like a man." The taunts eventually led to muzzle flashes from the American guns. The Japanese, now knowing where the Americans were, answered with murderous machine gun fire and hand grenades.

Finally, unhappy with the lack of progress on New Georgia, MacArthur dispatched Major General Oscar Griswold, Commander of XIV Corps, to take personal charge of the fight. Joining Griswold as his newly promoted Chief of Staff was Colonel Hugh Milton. Another Aggie and an ex-student of Milton's, Lieutenant Jack Horne (San Jon, '42) joined the 43rd as a combat engineer at Munda in September 1943. To help Griswold further, elements of the 37th and 25th Army Divisions and Admiral William 'Bull' Halsey's Navy were committed. They would be there for months before the stubborn Japanese were finally defeated. In the end, it took 40,000 allied troops to defeat the incredibly tough Japanese force.

Despite the bitterness of the campaign and the slow progress, a number of important lessons were learned in combating Japanese jungle tactics and pillbox fortifications—lessons that had not been learned even on Guadalcanal. These skills would be put to good use during the upcoming battles in the western Solomons and New Guinea and other islands that lay on the strategic 'island ladder' to Japan.

In the Central Pacific, Admiral Nimitz's forces would use a more direct approach—frontal amphibious assaults by the Marines on the Gilbert, Marshall, and Mariana Islands. A number of ex-Aggies were involved in those fights, and several died—Sergeant William T. Atchley (Grenville, '41) at Eniwetok; Seaman Second Class Fred G. Crawford (Roswell, '43) on the carrier *Liscome Bay*; and Private Otho W. Holtzclaw (House, '42) in the Gilberts.

Holtzclaw, an infantryman with the 2nd Marine Division, was killed during the brutal fight for Tarawa in November 1943. Color movies of the bloody Tarawa struggle, for the first time largely uncensored, shocked the American public with vivid scenes of the horrors of war. American Marines died by the hundreds. The movie showed their bodies bobbing in the bloody water and stacked on the beaches like cordwood. Japanese defenders in the heavily reinforced bunkers and pillboxes died by the thousands. The devastation of Tarawa was ghastly. Hardly a palm tree was left standing. Destroyed amtracs, tanks, steel drums, concrete debris, and charred human bodies were spewed about in a monstrous cratered wasteland. It was as if Hell had arisen in the Central Pacific. The vicious fighting on Tarawa cast a foreboding shadow on Admirals Nimitz, Halsey, and Spruance who would be faced with dislodging the maniacal Japanese from their strongholds at Kwajelein, Eniwetok, Tinian, Saipan, Guam, Peleliu, and Iwo Jima.

Meanwhile, back in the southwest Pacific, Captain Henry Gustafson returned to the War as a member of the 1st Marine Division, already a legendary unit because of its exploits on Guadalcanal. After surviving the sinking on the *Lexington* in the Coral Sea and returning to the U.S. to marry Caroline, Gustafson had volunteered for 'fleet duty' with the Marines. In spring 1943, he was assigned to the 1st Marine Division headquartered near Melbourne, but with elements of the Division training on New Caledonia more than 1,000 miles to the northeast. At the time, the Division was under MacArthur's Army command rather than the Navy. Stories to the contrary, MacArthur liked the Marines, especially the 1st Marine Division because of their superb record on Guadalcanal. Gustafson was in charge of two companies that were in training on New Caledonia. As he recalled,

> *I had no idea that he* [MacArthur] *and his staff would ever come and see me and my two little companies there, but they did. He was in his beautiful khaki outfit ... . He asked me all sorts of questions about the men, what their training was, what their attitude was, and how they were getting along. Sometimes he asked the same questions again. I do not know how important my answers were, but I gave him the same answers.*

The Marines continued training on New Caledonia until, in July 1943, the rested and reconditioned 1st Division received a directive. They were ordered to land at Cape Gloucester on the extreme western tip of New Britain, some 400 miles west of the Japanese stronghold at Rabaul. Although MacArthur, Admiral Halsey, and General Kenney were about to make the momentous decision to bypass Rabaul, the airfield at Cape Gloucester was critical to protect the backside of the allied move up the New Guinea coast. The Cape Gloucester operation would occur some five months later beginning on Christmas Day 1943.

In August 1943, chaffing after months in training in Australia, Tom Esterbrook and the 503rd Parachute Infantry were moved to a bivouac area near Port Moresby on the southeastern tip of New Guinea. After a bloody campaign, MacArthur's forces had recently secured Buna and Gona on the southeastern coast of New Guinea across the Owen Stanley Mountains from Port Moresby. Now MacArthur was ready for the next step up the ladder. In his words:

My plan to advance in northeast New Guinea and to seize the Houn Peninsula was entrusted to what was called the New Guinea Force. It was largely composed of Australian troops under the command of General Blamey. My order to the Force was to seize and occupy the sector that contained Salamaua, Lae, Finschafen, and Madang. Lae was to be the first main objective—its capture would breach the vital gate to the Houn Peninsula.

On September 4th, the attack on Lae was launched by the Australians moving along the coast to strike from the east. At the same time, another Australian column was being prepared to fly in overland ... . The success of the second column depended upon the seizure of an unused prewar airfield at Nadzab. With this field in our possession ... we could land troops, close the gap, and completely envelop Lae and the enemy forces there.

It was a delicate operation involving the first major parachute jump in the Pacific War. The unit to make the jump was the US 503rd Parachute Regiment. I inspected them and found, as was only natural, a sense of nervousness among the ranks. I decided that it would be advisable for me to fly in with them. I did not want them to go through their first baptism of fire without such comfort as my presence might bring to them. But they did not need me.

Three days before the operation, the enlisted troops of the 503rd had not yet been informed of their mission. But they knew they were going somewhere, and soon. Their officers had been holding not-so-secret meetings, and dozens of C-47 transports were arriving on the Port Moresby airstrip. On September 4th, one day before the drop, the men were assembled and briefed on the Lae-Nadzab operation.

The morning of September 5th dawned with drizzle and fog, aborting the planned 0530 departure across the Owen Stanley Mountains. Tom Esterbrook and his 503rd mates waited nervously. At 0730 the fog and rain let up. With parachutes and eighty pounds of combat gear, the troops climbed onto the C-47s. Within thirty minutes 1700 men were airborne. General George Kenney's 5th Air Force had formed a mighty armada of planes to support the Lae operation. It included six squadrons of B-25s, each with eight 50-caliber machine guns and 120 fragmentation bombs. The B-25s would strafe the drop zones minutes before the jump. Smoke-laying A-20s would follow the B-25s to lay smoke screens to protect the descending paratroopers from snipers. Above the 300 transports, bombers, and attack aircraft were three armed B-17s—one carrying General Kenney, one with General MacArthur, and the third for added protection. Then came six P-47s to provide topside cover. The Japanese did not challenge the awesome armada.

At 1015 the C-47s descended to 500 feet for the jump onto the Nadzab airfield. They came in three columns of 28 planes each. Within ten minutes Tom Esterbrook and the entire regiment was on the ground. It was a picture perfect operation. High above, MacArthur was watching and, as General Kenney described it, "jumping up and down like a kid." Later, at Port Moresby, MacArthur told Kenney that the jump was "the most perfect example of training and discipline he had ever witnessed." His concept of 'vertical envelopment' using airborne troops had met its first test.

On the ground, the astonished Japanese put up only light resistance. But three paratroopers were killed on the jump, two due to malfunctioning chutes, one who landed in a tall tree and fell to his death. Thirty-three others were injured in the jump. Eight men were killed and twelve wounded in later ground action against the Japanese.

Within a few days the Nadzab airstrip was secured and the Australian engineers were busy making it ready for allied planes. By September 14, 1943, Lae had fallen and the 503rd was soon sent back to Port Moresby. MacArthur sent a heartfelt telegram to Colonel Kenneth E. Kinsler, Commander of the 503rd, praising him and his men for the fine operation. The men were jubilant. But the glow of victory was short lived. Tragedy struck the Regiment when, inexplicably, Colonel Kinsler committed suicide in a gravel pit near the 503rd base camp in Port Moresby. The men felt depressed and abandoned. They were without their commander and stuck at steaming Port Moresby with lousy food, precious little beer, swarms of mosquitoes, and no contact with the war raging up New Guinea. In the chaos that followed, feelings grew raw among the men of the 503rd. Tom Esterbrook got into an altercation with a senior officer, then fell ill with a high fever. His illness became an excuse for his shipment back to Australia, first for hospitalization, then for duty in a regimental support role that would last the remainder of the War. The morale of the 503rd deteriorated further when several combat missions—drops near Rabaul and Cape Gloucester—were canceled. Now the 503rd seemingly had no mission.

Although Esterbrook and the 503rd would not be going to Cape Gloucester, Aggies, Henry Gustafson and Mert Gillis of the 1st Marine Division would. In the weeks before Christmas 1943, they were staging for the Cape Gloucester landing by practicing amphibious tactics in Milne Bay on the southeastern tip of New Guinea, 400 miles from Port Moresby.

One night, Mert Gillis heard Tokyo Rose on the radio, speaking in flawless, "sexy English" and playing the hit recordings of the popular swing bands—Glenn Miller, Benny Goodman, Artie Shaw, Tommy and Jimmy Dorsey. The songs were followed by 'news flashes' intended to rattle the Americans. That night one of the 'flashes' was ...

This gang of degenerates, cutthroats, and assorted jailbirds has been thrown out of Melbourne because of their misconduct and are now staging off northern New Guinea. Sometime during the week between Christmas and New Year's, they will attempt to invade the Cape Gloucester area of New Britain. I am pleased to add that our soldiers are fully prepared to repulse this insolent attempt. The jungles will run red with the blood of the butchers of Guadalcanal.

Tokyo Rose was right about the timing of Cape Gloucester, but little else. When the Marines landed a few days later the headlines of the Melbourne Herald proclaimed "OUR MARINES INVADE NEW BRITAIN!"

At 3 a.m. on Christmas morning, 1943, the 1st Marine Division made ready to land. A thunderous salvo of Naval guns opened up on the landing beach, which in actuality was not a beach, but a narrow shoreline overhung by vegetation, backed by swamp. General Kenney's "gang of gangsters," the 5th Army Air Force, blasted the area with 2,000 tons of explosives and murderously strafed the 'beach.' But the Japanese defenders were well inland, relatively safe from the bombardment. By 8:30 a.m., 2,500 Marines were ashore virtually unopposed. Their 'landing luck,' so welcome on Guadalcanal, still held.

But like Guadalcanal, things would soon change. Under General Hori Matsuda, the Japanese put up a horrific, if unorganized, fight. Although the prized airfield was captured on December 29th, the Japanese fought on using the now familiar tactics of sniping from trees, night infiltration, banzai charges, and clever concealment in camouflaged, below-ground pillboxes and bunkers. But the Marines had the new Sherman tank that was death on enemy pillboxes. By March 1944, the Marines had totally secured the Cape Gloucester area.

Gustafson's unit, the 2nd Battalion, 5th Regiment was held in reserve during the early part of the operation, but soon got their share of the swamps, jungles, and Japanese snipers. Later, in the last operation on New Britain, they were involved in a tough amphibious landing and battle at Talasea some 100 miles east of the original Cape Gloucester beachhead. Embarking in a 'rag-tag' Naval convoy, their only air support was a Piper Cub that dropped hand grenades on the Talasea beachhead. 'Naval gunfire' came from Sherman tanks firing from the LCM landing craft. They landed on March 6, 1944 under heavy Japanese mortar fire. The 5th Regiment pushed forward toward the main Japanese position on Mt. Schleuchter, which was captured three days later.

Despite the fear and excitement of his first land combat, Henry Gustafson talked more about the horrible weather, swamps, and mosquitoes—and how much his men liked being temporarily headquartered in a plantation that had rosewood furniture and, best of all, a "three-holer carved out of rosewood." Aggies and Marines always have their priorities right.

The Cape Gloucester campaign resulted in 311 Marine deaths and more than a thousand wounded. Estimates of Japanese dead ranged from 5,000 to 10,000. But mysteriously, thousands more, including General Matsuda, simply vanished. Undoubtedly, many committed suicide in the jungle and were never seen again.

With New Britain secure, MacArthur wanted the 1st Marine Division to stay on the island under his control. Admiral Nimitz reminded MacArthur that the Division was a Navy unit and that was where they belonged. Nimitiz won the argument. After more than two months in the jungle, the 1st Marine Division looked forward to a rest—as they put it, it was time to once again fight 'The Battle of Melbourne.' They loved Australia and the Aussies loved them. Unbelievably, the Navy shipped them to a new base camp at Pavuvu, barely 60 miles from Guadalcanal in the Russell Island chain. Some groused that it was the Navy's way of punishing them for having served under MacArthur.

A lucky, but deserving group of the Division's 260 officers and 4,600 enlisted men did not have to stay long on Pavuvu. They were being rotated home, and Corporal Mert Gillis was among them. As they were loading onto the transport ship, the Division band played a medley of popular hits and the departing men danced and laughed as they came aboard. But when the band broke into "From the Halls of Montezuma," the men wept openly. They had been through a lot together and no one who was there would ever forget it. By summer 1944, Gillis was back in Las Cruces and State College where he had a joyful reunion with his wife, the former Sis Campbell. Sis's brother Jack Campbell, also Gillis' ex-classmate, was at that moment on Bougainville fighting the Japanese who were still resisting in the jungle.

Bougainville, the largest of the Solomon Islands, was invaded by American forces commanded by Admiral Halsey on November 1, 1943. Heavily guarded by 400,000 Japanese troops, the big island and its many enemy airstrips were vital to the overall goal of taking Rabaul and 'moving up the ladder' toward New Guinea, the Philippines, and eventually, Japan itself.

The initial landings on Bougainville bypassed the most heavily guarded installations at Buka and Bonis near the southern end of the island where Jack Lee had been killed during a bombing raid a year earlier. Instead, Halsey's forces landed at Empress Augusta Bay, halfway up Bougainville's west coast. The landing caught the small Japanese garrison by surprise, and they fled into the jungle. Soon a new American airstrip was in operation and a strong defensive perimeter put into position.

Helping to man that perimeter was the Americal Division and Aggie Lieutenant Jack Campbell, who had arrived in November with Colonel Hugh Milton and General George Griswold, overall commander of the XIV Corps. Soon, planes from the new Bougainville air base joined those from the carriers *Saratoga* and *Princeton* that had been blasting the big Japanese base at Rabaul. One of the pilots on those raids was Jack Durio who had earlier flown bombing missions in support of both the New Georgia and Bougainville landings. Durio remembers seeing the desperate rush from Simpson Harbor at Rabaul by the Japanese destroyers and cruisers as he and and the other American flyers came in. By mid-November 1943, reconnaissance flights showed Simpson Harbor clear of ships. The Japanese, all but conceding defeat in the Solomons, had pulled their Navy back from Rabaul to Truk, 800 miles to the north.

On Bougainville, Jack Campbell was in charge of an infantry patrol that had the dirty job of ferreting out the 'Japanese jungle bunnies' that were constantly probing the American defensive perimeter. As in earlier campaigns on Guadalcanal and New Georgia, the Japanese proved to be adept, crafty jungle fighters, especially at night. An Associated Press news dispatch described Campbell's patrol as 'Kampbell's Kool Killers.' It was termed the "best patrol outfit on Bougainville." It seemed an unlikely role for Jack Campbell who back at State College before the War had gulped down dozens of malts and bananas to gain enough weight to meet the Army's minimum requirements for a commission. Campbell and his men fought together for months in the terrifying jungles, and dispatched scores of Japanese to early meetings with the Emperor.

In March 1944, Campbell and the Americal Division also fought in a major battle to repulse a suicide attack by some 15,000 Japanese who had infiltrated by land from the south. The Americal and 37th Divisions held, killing more than 8,000 of the enemy. The battle proved to be the last major action in the Solomons. Soon thereafter, a major resupply and staging effort began on Bougainville. It was then that Colonel Hugh Milton assembled Jack Campbell, Jim Baird, Mark Radoslovich, Mansil Scrivner, and Otis Horton for the famous 'New Mexicans in the Pacific' photo that was seen in many New Mexico newspapers. This group of Aggies (save Radoslovich who would land on Luzon with the 43rd Division in February 1945) would serve with elements of the 93rd Division in operations on Green Island, several bases in New Guinea and on Mindanao, Philippines. It was all part of MacArthur's move 'up the ladder' toward Japan.

ROTC Days

(1)

(2)

(1) Colonel Alexander Chilton, Head of the Military Science (ROTC) program at New Mexico A&M for many years before and during World War II. (2) Sergeant Jack 'Sarge' Cragin, long-time chief NCO in the New Mexico A&M ROTC program. (3) New Mexico A&M Military Science staff, mid 1930s. *l. to r.* Cragin, Fletcher, Hallowell, Thompson. (Photos courtesy: NMSU Alumni Association.)

(3)

(1)

(1) Cheerleader Hubert Jeffus with Gloria Hayner *(l.)* and Letha Glee Wall. (2) ROTC cadets Jack Horne *(l.)* and Harold 'Red' Howell. Horne, 43rd Division, received the Silver Star for gallantry during the battle for Ipo Reservoir outside Manila in Spring 1945. (3) New Mexico A&M rifle team, 1939. Bill Porter is at upper right. (Courtesy: NMSU Alumni Association.)

(2)

(3)

(1)

(2)

(1) ROTC Color Guard. Pecos Finley is second from left with American flag. (2) ROTC cadet officers. Tom Esterbrook is center front. (Photos courtesy: NMSU Alumni Association.)

(3) By late 1942, NM A&M was on a full 'war footing.' War Bond Drives included the Las Cruces High School band, ROTC cadets, and the local American Legion. (4) Intensified ROTC training at A&M included 'heroic' publicity shots. (Photos courtesy: NMSU Alumni Association.)

(3)

(4)

The 200th Coast Artillery (AA)

Happier Days – (1) *USS Coolidge* docking in Manila with New Mexico's 200th Coast Artillery, October 1941. The *Coolidge* was later sunk by a Japanese submarine off Espiritu Santo, New Hebrides, in December 1942. (US Army photo) (2) Captains Gerald Greeman and Hubert Jeffus on the *Coolidge* deck. (Courtesy: New Mexico Magazine) (3) The 200th Coast Artillery loading onto buses in Manila for the trip to Clark Field, October 1941. (Courtesy: New Mexico Magazine)

(1)

(2)

(3)

Approximately 1400 of the 1800 members of the 200th Coast Artillery (AA) were from New Mexico. Many were alumni of A&M or had attended for short periods. Another 400 New Mexico men, women, and children were captured as members of other branches of the armed forces or were civilian internees. Because of the large number of New Mexicans captured in the Philippines, New Mexico had the dubious distinction of having the highest per capita of Japanese POWs/Civilian Internees of any state in the United States. (Photographs on this and the following two pages were obtained from NM A&M yearbooks, courtesy of the NMSU Alumni Association, and *Heroes of Bataan, Corregidor, and Northern Luzon*, by Marcus Griffin.)

Robert Amy

Ernest J. Armijo

Byron C. Beal

Dow Bond

Edward E. Chavez

James W. Donaldson

John W. Farley

John R. Flowers

Anthony R. George

Rey F. Gonzales

Gerald B. Greeman

Richard B. Hunt

George H. Huston

Hubert P. Jeffus

James B. Jones

Robert J. Knight

Jack S. Lewis

Thomas V. Long

William E. Love

Solly Manasse

Charles R. Nunn

David M. Nunn

Arnold A. Orosco

Thomas M. Palmer

Robert J. Remondini

Andrew J. Robinson

J. Dallas Thorpe

Phil Witherspoon

Paul F. Womack

Foster W. Zimmerman

Other Aggies in the Philippines

New Mexico Aggie NIT basketball team at Jack Dempsey's Restaurant, New York City, March 1939. Six members went to war. Clockwise from front row left, Mel Ritchey (Hale Center, TX, '40) flew fifty B-17 missions in Africa and Mediterranean, Angie Cunico (Raton, '41) killed in air training accident off Florida. Otis Horton ('41) served in Solomons and New Guinea with 93rd Division, Kiko Martinez (El Paso, '39) Army Corp of Engineers in New Mexico, Pecos Finley ('39), and 'Pucker' Wood ('39) was with the 43rd Division in the Solomons and Philippines.

One of the Aggie Greats, Pecos Uvalde Finley (Causey, '39) was a star basketball player, ROTC graduate, and popular student. He flew to the Philippines on the 'China Clipper' in August 1941, to be Quartermaster officer with the Philippine Scouts. He died as a POW at Camp O'Donnell on June 1, 1942. (Photos courtesy: NMSU Alumni Association.)

The McCorkle twins of Las Cruces in their graduation year, 1932. Robert Roy (*insert*) served as an Army officer in Europe during World War II. John Ray (*above left*), who served as Senior Class President, was an Army Air Corps officer sent to the Philippines in 1941. Without planes, he and his men became de facto infantry and he was killed during the Battle of the Pockets. Although not the first Aggie death of the war, he was the first killed in the Philippines. His wife, Nellie Starr McCorkle, of Hatch, became the first Aggie war widow. (Photos courtesy: NMSU Alumni Association.)

William 'Wild Bill' Porter (Las Cruces, '41) as an Aggie. He was an ROTC cadet and received the Silver Star for heroism as an infantry officer in the Philippines. His actions were immortalized in the War Gum Card shown below. Porter survived an incredible ordeal in Japanese POW camps and 'hell ships.' (Photos courtesy: Porter Family.)

Albert B. Fall Chase

William N. Foster

Francis B. Powell

J. J. Valdenaar

Charles R. Sparks

Aggies served in many different Army units in the Philippines. All shown here died as POWs, either in camps or on 'hell ships.' (Photos courtesy: NMSU Alumni Association.)

Surrender of Filamerican forces at Bataan on April 9, 1942, and the beginning of the infamous Death March. (Japanese photo.)

William A. Trogstad

Over the Pacific

Leo M. Eminger

Billy D. Hunter

Lisle Foord

Eminger was lost in his B-17 over the Solomons, in October 1942; Hunter's plane was shot down in the South Pacific, August 1943; Foord died over Vella Lavella Island, Solomons, in August 1944. *(below)* Lt. Jack Lee, 11th Heavy Bombardment Group, 13th Air Force, fought at Midway and was one of the earliest Army pilots to fight at Guadalcanal and in other Solomon battles. He co-piloted with Major James Edmundson *(below r.)* on many missions before he was shot down and killed in the lead plane during the November 18, 1942, Bougainville attack. Lee was post-humously awarded the Silver Star. (Photos courtesy: NMSU Alumni Association. *Bottom right* US Army photo.)

Jack Lee

Robert Hedley

James S. Quesenberry

James Toliver

James M. Wilkerson

Hedley, stationed on the *USS Langley*, was killed January 22, 1945, when a Japanese bomb hit the officer's stateroom. Quesenberry was lost over the South Pacific in May 1944. Toliver died in a bombing raid over Tokyo in February 1945. Wilkerson was killed in an air training accident in Hawaii, June 1943. (Photos courtesy: NMSU Alumni Association.)

During the invasion of Luzon, Navy Lieutenant Gerald Thomas attacked the Japanese by air from the carrier *USS Essex*. Thomas would become an Aggie in 1970 as the seventeenth president of New Mexico State University. (Photo courtesy: Gerald Thomas.)

B-17, the 'Flying Fortress' over the Solomons

Jack Durio

Durio flew numerous bombing missions in the Pacific during battles at New Georgia, Bougainville, Rabaul, Iwo Jima, Okinawa, and mainland Japan. He was awarded two Distinguished Flying Crosses, the Navy Cross, and other air medals. (Photo courtesy: Jack Durio.)

Carr was killed in action over Japan, July 9, 1943. McLaughlin died in action over Central Pacific, January 22, 1944. Ortiz was lost over Ellice Island in January 1944. (Photos courtesy: NMSU Alumni Association.)

Robert L. Carr

Paul McLaughlin

Ralph P. Ortiz

Mert Gillis

Jim Meadows

Gillis, Aggie halfback, fought with the 1st Marine Division on Guadalcanal and Cape Gloucester. (Photo courtesy: NMSU Alumni Assoc.)

Meadows served on the *USS Breton* and *USS Lardner*. He was witness to surrender ceremonies on the battleship *Missouri*. (Photo courtesy: Jim Meadows.)

Billups was the first Aggie to die at sea when he was killed in action on the cruiser *USS Augusta*, in November 1942, during the Battle of Savo Island off Guadalcanal. Sturman saw duty on the carrier *USS Copohee* throughout the South Pacific. Holtzclaw was killed in action in the Gilbert Islands, during January 1944. (Photos courtesy: NMSU Alumni Assoc.)

Charles Billups

Bill Sturman

Otho W. Holtzclaw

J. Henry Gustafson   (1)

USS Lexington   (2)

Marine Captain Gustafson, survived the sinking of the *USS Lexington* during the Battle of the Coral Sea. He led a 1st Marine Division company and battalion in battles at Cape Gloucester and Peleliu. He was wounded on Okinawa in April 1945. (Courtesy: NMSU Alumni Assoc.) (2) Crewmen leave the damaged *Lexington* on May 8, 1942. (3) 1st Marine Division, with Aggies Gustafson and Gillis, lands at Cape Gloucester. (4) 1st Marine Division in Battle of Peleliu where Gustafson earned the Silver Star for leading a highly successful assault on neighboring Ngesebus Island. (Photos: US Navy.)

(3)

(4)

Aggies at Bougainville. This famous photo features *(l. to r.)* Captain Jim Baird, Captain Otis Horton, Colonel Hugh Milton, Lieutenant Jack Campbell, Captain Mansil Scrivner, and Captain Mark Radoslovich. All except Milton (President on leave) were the product of the NM A&M ROTC program. (Photo courtesy: NMSU Alumni Assoc.)

Jack Cambell

Jim Baird

Dangerous jungle patrol work like this (*below*) was undertaken by Jack Campbell's men. 'Kampbell's Kool Killers,' were described in an AP dispatch as the "best patrol outfit on Bougainville." (US Army)

Ex-Aggie halfback Jim Baird, like Horton, Scrivner, and Radoslovich, were mainstays in the massive supply effort in the Solomons and New Guinea that moved U.S. forces up the ladder to the Philippines and Okinawa. (Photos courtesy: NMSU Alumni Assoc.)

ala 'Kampbell's Kool Killers'

American forces landing at Bougainville, November 1, 1943. (US Army)

Otis Horton

Ex-Aggie basketballer Otis Horton saw duty with the 93rd Division in the Solomons and New Guinea. Esterbrook was an officer with the 503rd Parachute Infantry Regiment that received a Presidential Unit Citation for action in New Guinea and the Philippines. (Photos courtesy: NMSU Alumni Assoc.)

Tom Esterbrook

Russell Islands, where on the Island of Pavuvu, Gustafson and the 1st Marine Division battled land crabs and rats, and saw the Bob Hope Show. (US Navy)

Baylus Cade

Mansil Scrivner

Michael Taylor

James 'Whiz' Bradford

Mark Radoslovich

Morris 'Pucker' Wood

Other Aggie officers instrumental in moving U.S. forces through the South and Central Pacific.

Retaking the Philippines & on to Japan

Lt. Col. Jesse Mechem

Jesse Mechem

Lt. Colonel Jesse Mechem was killed by enemy fire while leading an infantry battalion of the 96th Division infantry battalion during the Battle of Leyte, October 29, 1944. His men erected a memorial and christened it 'Mechem Ridge.' He was posthumously awarded the Silver Star for gallantry. (Photos courtesy: NMSU Alumni Assoc.)

'Mechem Ridge'

Walter Fite   C. Quentin Ford

Fite and Freeman landed on Leyte with the 96th
Infantry Division. Gallagher and Gerhart landed north
of the 96th with the 1st Cavalry Division. C. Quention
Ford served on the *USS Libra,* an attack cargoship,
throught the Pacific. Gerhart later won the Distinguished Service Cross for his actions on Luzon.
Shields, a Marine sergeant was killed by enemy fire
during the Leyte landing on October 20, 1944. Horne,
with the 43rd Division, went on to win the Silver Star
for his actions during the battle for Ipo Dam on Luzon.
(Photos courtesy: NMSU Alumni Assoc.)

Carl Freeman   James C. Gerhart

Francis Gallagher   Robert T. Shields   Jack Horne

Colonel Hugh M. Milton, III

New Mexico A&M President Hugh M. Milton III, was a Lt. Col. reserve officer in the Army Chemical Corps when war broke out in 1941. With the liberation of Manila, Milton, as Chief of Staff for XIV Corps Commander General Oscar Griswold, was in charge of bringing food and supplies to the starving inmates of Santo Tomas and Bilibid Prisons.
(Photos courtesy: NMSU Alumni Assoc.)

A regal General Douglas MacArthur on Luzon shortly after the American landing. (US Army)

The massive American landing at Lingayen Gulf, Luzon, January 9. 1945. (US Army)

George Gray, a Los Banos POW camp inmate, led secret efforts to coordinate a daring rescue of 2,100 inmates by American paratroopers and Filipino guerillas on February 18, 1945.
(Photo courtesy: NMSU Alumni Assoc.)

(1)

(2)

1st Cavalry soldiers escort Japanese guards out of liberated Santo Tomas prison. (US Army)

(1) Supplying the liberated Bilibid Prison by air, was an operation supervised by Col. Milton. (2) Bilibid Prison, February 1945. General MacArthur reviewed the ill inmates as they stood by their beds. (3) American paratroopers of the 503rd Parachute Infantry surprised the Japanese forces on Corregidor with their daring drop on February 16, 1945. (Photos: US Army) (4) As Santo Tomas was liberated, an errant shell hit the compound, killing Robert McFie, Jr. Robert and Dorothy McFie were inmates of Santo Tomas for three long years. (Photo courtesy: NMSU Alumni Assoc.)

(4)

(3)

The *Oryoku Maru* was the last of the infamous 'hell ships,' and its passengers probably suffered the most. Of ten known Aggies on this voyage, four died. (Courtesy: *Heroes of Bataan*).

The A-bomb mushroomed over Nagasaki on August 9, 1945. A view of devastated Nagasaki after the bomb. Captain (Dr.) John Farley of the 200th ministered to the inmates and Japanese guards wounded by the atomic blast. Forty-eight POWs died. (US Army)

Nagasaki Bomb

Post-bomb Nagasaki

Iwo Jima, Ulithi, and Okinawa

Wright, a forward air observer, 5th Marine Division, was killed on Iwo Jima, February 24, 1945. Ortiz, a Marine, fought the caved Japanese on Iwo Jima with flamethrower and grenades. He was killed in action on March 1, 1945, and received the Navy Cross. (Photos courtesy: NMSU Alumni Assoc.)

Warren Wright

Robert Ortiz

(1)

(1) Marines of the 5th Division perservered under murderous Japanese crossfire on Iwo Jima. Mount SurIbachi is to the left. (US Marine Corps) (2) The massive American fleet anchorage at Ulithi Lagoon. (US Navy) (3) The pleasures of Mog Mog, Ulithi Lagoon where US personnel were permitted R&R. The officers here are being entertained by a band of black enlisted men. (US Navy)

(2)

(3)

New Mexico correspondent Ernie Pyle moved to the Pacific Theater after a distinguished service reporting the war in Europe. He came ashore with Henry Gustafson's 1st Marine Division on Okinawa and was killed during combat on the small Okinawan Island of Le Shima. (US Army)

Gunnery officer on the destroyer *Longshaw*, Gray was killed by Japanese shellfire off the coast of Okinawa on May 18, 1945. He was posthumously awarded the Bronze Star. Skipworth was a combat intelligence officer with the 7th Army Division and died in action on Okinawa, April 5, 1945. He received the Silver Star for his action on Kwajleiin. (Photos courtesy: NMSU Alumni Assoc.)

Correspondent Ernie Pyle

Edward Gray   Roy Skipworth

Marine Corporal Eakens was killed in action on Iwo Jima, March 8, 1945.

Resistance was light when American forces first landed on Okinawa, April 1, 1945, but turned brutal as Army and Marine troops moved south where the Japanese were entrenched. (US Army)

William A. Eakens

American Landing Forces at Okinawa

It's Over

American POWs in Japan celebrate their freedom in August 1945. Jim Meadows, on the destroyer *Lardner*, saw duty in ferrying allied POWs to central staging areas in Japan. (Courtesy: *The Retired Officer,* September 1977) General Douglas MacArthur greets a gaunt General Anthony Wainwright in Tokyo a few days after Wainwright's liberation from a POW camp in Manchuria (US Army)

General MacArthur and Admiral Chester Nimitz approach the 'surrender desk' aboard the battleship *Missouri* in Tokyo Bay, September 2, 1945. (US Navy)

V-J Parade in Honolulu, September 1945. Gerald Greeman, newly liberated POW was designated one of the 'Heroes of Bataan,' and among those honored by the festivities. (US Army)

This is what it's all about, reunion with family and friends! Bill Porter and sister Winnie Porter Marshall Price in El Paso in November 1945, after Porter's release from a POW camp in Manchuria. (Photo courtesy: Porter Family)

PELELIU

The last major action planned before the Philippine invasion was the capture of Peleliu, a heavily fortified Japanese bastion in the Palau Island group about 500 miles east of Mindanao. The 1st Marine Division was given the assignment, and despite the dread of facing the Japanese again, they were ready. By August 1944, Gustafson and the 1st Marine Division had definitely had more than enough of Pavuvu.

Pavuvu had come to mean many things to the Marines, none of them dear to the heart—utter isolation, muggy heat, mosquitoes, giant land crabs, and voracious rats. When the Division arrived there was virtually nothing to meet the needs of the men—no roads, no water system, no housing, no electricity. They spent the first few months building everything from scratch. They slept in mildew-infested 'Army reject' tents salvaged from Guadalcanal. A young private, an Iowa farm boy who knew of such things, said living in the tents "reminded me of a smelly barnyard swamped with dung and cow piss."

The land crabs of Pavuvu had a blue black body with sharp bristles and spines covering 6-inch crooked legs. They were flat ugly. In his book *Peleliu, Tragic Triumph*, Bill Ross described the crabs and their cousins in misery, the rats.

> *No one ever figured out how many of them* [land crabs] *inhabited Pavuvu, but the number probably was in the hundreds of thousands. The hordes hid by day, roamed everywhere at night, and took refuge wherever they found themselves at dawn. Before putting on his boondocks boots in the morning, everyone on the island violently shook them to make sure one of the slumbering vermin hadn't taken up temporary residence.*
>
> *Meandering battalions of land crabs were troublesome problems to jeep drivers, especially during the twice-monthly mating rituals of the varmints. Massed thousands covered stretches of roads and were flattened under the*

vehicles' wheels, creating a gooey mess that was as difficult to navigate as a deep mudhole.

... Forget the rats? Impossible! Some of the evil-looking long-toothed, snarling rodents were 2 feet long from fiendishly pointed snoot to whiplike tail. They were an indefatigable foe in the endless struggle of fury and frustration waged mainly at night .... Come dusk and they were on the move, marching as armies in tight formation on the tops of tents, their feet rat-tat-tat-tatting like drumbeats on the taut canvas. They would slide down the ropes and charge through the tents, screeching loud and belligerent battle cries as they went in a determined search for food.

The Marines tried everything. The medical detachment smeared the bottoms of trees with cyanide. The poison worked well, too well. Every day there were countless thousands of dead rats. Large work parties spent hours collecting and burying the vile creatures. One desperate battalion commander ordered flamethrower attacks which killed more than 400 one night. But the armies of rats kept coming. Finally, the mass eradication efforts were abandoned as useless.

But individually, the men came up with ingenious methods to assert some control of their individual tents. Henry Gustafson's rattrap was a marvel of revenge. Just outside his tent, he buried a 5-gallon Wesson oil can, leaving the top open and protruding an inch above ground level. Because of the frequent rains, the can always had a foot or so of water in the bottom. A date was loosely tied on a string that dangled invitingly a few inches into the middle of the can. Every night at least one rat would lurch for the date. Rat and date would then fall with a loud plop into the water a few feet below. The men in the tent smiled with satisfaction as they heard the rat's frantic dog paddling and scratching gradually slow down, then cease entirely in about an hour as it drowned.

Jungle rot and ringworm began to infest the troops. Bill Ross recalled that "Morning sick call ... looked like a strange nudist camp in a coconut grove." There were hundreds of buck naked Marines painting each other's buttocks with Methiolate to combat ringworm infections. Many became so sick they were evacuated to the fully equipped Navy hospital on Banika Island, twenty miles away. Mental illness, deep depression, and island fever were common. There were several suicide cases and many fights.

The men needed hope and, miraculously, that is what they got. The Bob Hope Show came to Pavuvu!

Hope's entourage included Jerry Colonna, complete with bulging eyes, handlebar mustache, and bullhorn voice. Tony Romano played guitar and was almost Hope's equal with the wise cracks. The sultry Frances Langford sang, and the gorgeous redheaded dancer, Patti Thomas made the Marines' eyes bulge like Colonna's. Hope's group arrived in a formation of military Piper Cubs, which flew from Banika through rainsqualls, landing on a coral jeep road. More than 10,000 men watched the show, performed on the bed of a big flatbed truck.

In one skit, Hope asked Colonna, posing as a German psychiatrist, "Dr. Dimchoff, there's something bothering these men. I can't quite put my finger on it. These guys need help. What can we do?"

Colonna looked at Hope, rolled his eyes and screeched, "Dat's eezy, you fool! Vhat dees men need is vomen! Thousans of dem!"

Amid hoots and whistles, out came Patti Thomas in a scanty costume. She danced a sizzling routine to the music of Tony Romano accompanied by four members of the Division band. Then came Frances Langford singing love songs and nostalgic ballads. Finally, Hope ended the show with "Thanks for the Memories." Many a tough Marine held back tears as Hope's group lifted off to return Banika. Some talked of "swimming home." It would be worth it, just to see another American woman.

But no Marines would be swimming home. Instead, in early September 1944 they left Pavuvu by transport ship for a 2,000-mile voyage to the northwest. The 1st Marine Division was soon to assault the Japanese bastion at Peleliu in the Palau Island group. Naval planners had long thought that the protection of the Philippine campaign required the capture of the Japanese base and airfields at Peleliu and Anguar Island, a few miles south. Many military historians now say that the invasion of Peleliu was unnecessary—that all the casualties could have been avoided, that Peleliu could have been bypassed without endangering the war effort. Now, in the 'keen light of hindsight,' perhaps these arguments were right. But the brave Marines who fought there will never forget the Battle of Peleliu, and they will never accept the notion that those who died or were wounded there fought in vain.

Colonel Kunio Nakagawa, the tough Japanese commander on Peleliu, had no intention of accepting defeat. General Sadae Inoue, in overall command of Japanese forces in the Palaus, entrusted Nakagawa with an elite force of more than 10,000 troops. Inoue told Nakagawa that he didn't want banzai charges. He wanted the application of "material power." "The Americans rely solely upon material power," he said. "If we repay them with material power it will shock them beyond imagination." Still, as if recognizing the outcome of the coming battle, Nakagawa and his men were instructed to fight and die to the last man. And that is what they did. And the Americans paid an awful price.

Peleliu, a coral island of six by three miles surrounded by a coral reef, is located about 500 miles east of the big Philippine Island of Mindanao. The southern portion with its prize airstrip was relatively flat and vegetated. It comprised coral, a large beach and an area of mangrove swamp. Running north were the Umburbrogol Mountains, a strange, uneven landscape of ridges and spires as high as 300 feet. The Umurbrogols were honey combed by old adits and tunnels from phosphate mining undertaken by the Japanese in previous decades. Nakagawa used the existing excavations and the eerie spires and hummocky coral ridges to build a fantastic network of interconnected bunkers and pillboxes. More than 500 improved caverns were constructed. Some had five or six levels with reinforced steel doors, retracting artillery on tracks, slotted gunports, and secret escape and entrance hatches. Nakagawa also emplaced more than 500 men with artillery on Ngesebus, a small island just north of the main island. From Ngesebus, the Japanese would shell and harass the Americans from the rear.

Nakagawa knew that the firepower of the U.S. warships and planes would not allow him to stop an amphibious landing. He planned to let the Americans land, and with his incredible firepower pre-zeroed in, inflict grave damage on the beachhead. Then, the entrenched Japanese in the higher terrain would counterattack the weakened Americans at an opportune point in the battle. Even if the counterattacks weren't successful, Nakagawa reasoned that the reinforced, bristling bunker complexes could sustain murderous fire and punishment on the Marines for weeks.

D-Day at Peleliu was September 15, 1944. For weeks prior to D-Day, General Kenney's 5th Air Force and Halsey's carrier based planes bombarded the island. Beginning on September 12th, Admiral Oldendorf's warships shelled Peleliu for three days, flattening all above ground installations. The Navy announced that they had "run out of targets." This led to grossly optimistic claims by some of the high-ranking officers that the landing would be a cakewalk.

The operation had problems from the start. The encircling coral reef, 500 yards offshore, required that the Marines be taken first from the troop ships by LST; then transferred in company-sized units to amtracs for the ride across the reef to the beaches. Despite smoke screens and machine gun fire from the landing craft, the Japanese shot up the slow-moving amtracs like ducks in a shooting gallery.

The 1st, 5th, and 7th Regiments of the 1st Division landed abreast along a mile-long beach next to the airfield. The plan was for the 1st Regiment to push directly toward the airfield. The 7th Regiment was to attack the entrenched Japanese to the south. Henry Gustafson with the 2nd Battalion of the 5th Marines was ordered to help the 7th with the securing of the airfield, then to push north to engage the heaviest concentration of Japanese in the Umburbrogol ridges.

Everyone who landed and lived through D-Day at Peleliu had his own version of Hell to tell. In *Peleliu: Tragic Triumph*, Bill Ross summarized a few first-hand accounts.

> *Horrible fear and mind-boggling bewilderment ... . Awful sights of blown-to-pieces corpses. Mortally wounded men grotesquely sprawled in screaming agony. Explosions louder than doomsday's thunder as artillery and mortar shells fell in torrents. A narrow strip of sand cluttered with the wreckage of destroyed vehicles. Men desperately pushing inland, darting from shell hole to shell hole to survive machine-gun fire and hand grenades that seemed to come from every direction.*

Forty-five years after D-Day, Navy doctor, Lieutenant Edward Hagan wrote a letter recalling his version of Hell on the beachhead as included by Ross in his book.

> *I can't imagine how anything could be worse. After more than forty years, there isn't a single day that I haven't thought about Peleliu ... . Horribly wounded Marines were staggering toward the beach, some apparently not wounded; not physically, but mentally out of it ... . There were geysers of water all around the incoming amtracs and many were burning on the beach and in the water. There is no way that one can exaggerate the intensity of the combined mortar, artillery, and small-arms fire ... .*

Some were so exhausted they had to be helped to walk. Some smiled eerily as if mocking death for being cheated. Some shuffled like zombies in a horror movie, their faces and uniforms covered in coral grime. For awhile, Gustafson and the 2nd Battalion, 5th Regiment were a little better off than the 1st and 7th Regiments. But there was virtually no cover for anyone and the crossfire continued into the afternoon of the 15th. By then, the 5th Marines had moved across the southern portion of the airfield and were encountering heavy enemy fire. And the 1st Regiment was completely pinned down and taking brutal casualties. The fortified Japanese on the south heavily engaged the 7th Marines. That afternoon, temperatures soared above 100 degrees. In the coming days, it would go above 115 degrees. A severe water shortage developed and many collapsed from heat exhaustion.

On D-Day plus one, September 16th, Bill Ross recounted Marine combat correspondent Sergeant Walter Conway's description of the scene with Gustafson's 2nd Battalion, 5th Regiment at a frontline command post. It was in huge shell crater twenty yards across with a pool of filthy, stagnant water and chunks of coral debris on the bottom.

> *... Huddled uncomfortably on one bank, seeking shade form the blistering sun and cover from Jap mortars, were Majors Richard T. Washburn of*

New Haven, Connecticut and John H. Gustafson of Las Cruces, New Mexico. Both were sweat-stained and weary from thirty hours under fire. Neither spoke. Mud-spattered enlisted men dotted the sides of the hole. Some dozed. Others gulped, moistened their lips with their tongues, and looked longingly at the bottom of the hole ... .

One exhausted, thirst-crazed Marine fell into the hole and drank deeply of the stagnant water. Japanese snipers were watching the Marines come in and out of the shell-hole. Bullets bit at the top of the hole, raising stinging coral dust and infuriating the men below. Finally, during a quiet interval, a Corporal Russell grabbed his rifle and crawled over the rim into the surrounding vegetation. Ten minutes later, those in the command post heard the familiar retort of a Marine carbine, then the chatter of a Japanese machine gun. They worried about Russell until, a few minutes later, he rolled smiling into the shell hole carrying a Nambu automatic rifle and a Japanese flag.

"The little yellow bastard didn't even have a canteen," Russell cussed. "And what the hell am I gonna do with this?" he said, holding up the Nambu.

Another Marine replied, "Take it back to headquarters and see if you can swap it for a couple of cans of water."

By twilight the smell of decaying Japanese bodies around the shell hole was unbearable. Huge bluebottle flies swarmed on the corpses, then lit all over the now bare backs of the Marines. The Marines were nearly delirious with thirst. Finally, a voice was heard over the Japanese machine guns and the buzzing flies.

"Water's up! Water's up! Two canteens a man. Come and get it!" It was 1st Lieutenant Layton Bailey of Dallas, Texas, leading a team of courageous black Marines that had spent the entire day under fire, bringing water and ammunition across the coral reef, through the water, and then to the front lines, all under the unrelenting Japanese crossfire. Bailey apologized for being late.

In the morning, Gustafson and his men were ordered to move up. The invisible Japanese sniped from trees, caves, and foxholes. The last to leave the shell hole was Corporal Charley Draper, of Athens, Georgia. He looked down and said, "Ah—Peleliu Spa." A few seconds later, a Japanese mortar landed dead center, and 'Peleliu Spa' was gone. Henry Gustafson's amazing luck had held once again.

The Marines, reinforced by the 321st Army Infantry Regiment, fought on day and night against fanatical Japanese resistance. Five days later, on September 22nd Gustafson was leading his men in action against the Umburbrogol ridges when he received word to report to

Regimental headquarters. He was congratulated and told that he was the new commanding officer of the 3rd Battalion, 5th Marine Regiment. The old CO had been wounded and was being evacuated. Before he had time to fully respond, Gustafson was told that the 3rd Battalion had a new mission—attack and secure the little island of Ngesebus due north of the main island of Peleliu. There, the Japanese held an airfield and had gun emplacements that were raining death on the Marines attempting to take the Umurbrogols.

The attack on Ngesebus occurred on September 28th, and it was one of the best tactical combat operations of the Pacific War. Bill Ross described the scene.

> *Ngesebus's tiny size—it was less than 2,500 yards long from tip to tip and about half that wide—was not indicative of its importance to the overall strategy for ultimate victory on Peleliu. In American hands ... Ngesebus would give U.S. troops control of northern Peleliu and thus isolate the Japanese in their dwindling and hard-pressed pocket in the Umburbrogols ... . Not only was the operation carried out as planned, but it was a classic textbook performance, a near-perfect display of how to coordinate and use all of the ingredients—naval, air, artillery, and ground troops—to pull off a combat landing with minimum losses.*

H-Hour was 9:00 a.m. on September 28th. At 8:00 a.m., Ngesebus was blasted by fire from the battleship *Mississippi* and the cruisers *Denver* and *Columbus*. At 8:40, the warships ceased firing and Corsair attack aircraft bombed and strafed the Japanese in an awesome display of treetop flying. At 9:05 a.m. Major Gustafson's battalion began the attack with thirteen amphibious Sherman tanks first in line, followed by troop-carrying amtracs. By 9:30 the entire attack force was ashore. The ferocious, clock-perfect attack sent the Japanese reeling. The Japanese commander later recounted that the operation had left him and his men stupefied.

In his understated way, Gustafson later described the action.

> *It should be emphasized that with the terrain most suitable for an infantry-tank attack, with both elements coordinating perfectly, the operation was made to appear easy. The tanks should get a great deal of credit, but, on the other hand, the tank commanders later said they never experienced such coordination from the infantry.*

97

As Bill Ross wrote,

> *The inescapable fact ... was that Ngesebus was defended by 500 well-led enemy troops, nearly all of them in caves and strongly prepared positions ... . To say that the 3rd Battalion of the 5th Marines lost "only" forty-eight troops—fifteen killed and thirty-three wounded—is to demean the devotion to duty and sacrifices made to take the piece of coral.*

The 3rd Battalion killed 440 of the Japanese troops and captured twenty-three after the landing. The Japanese casualties were the heaviest inflicted by one battalion in any single engagement during the Battle for Peleliu. Within a day, Gustafson's men on Ngesebus were relieved by the Army's 321st Regimental Combat Team and returned to the main island of Peleliu. Gustafson was awarded the Silver Star, but he did not have much time to contemplate the medal. In a few days, he and his men were back in action again in the brutal fighting to dislodge the Japanese from the Umurbrogols. The caves were assaulted one by one with flamethrowers, grenades, and carbines.

Before Peleliu was over in early October, Gustafson had lost forty pounds and many of his men. But Colonel Kunio Nakagawa and his fanatical Japanese troops had been annihilated. On the last day in his cave, Nakagawa tearfully burned the regimental colors and shot himself in the head shortly after he had radioed Tokyo, "It is all over on Peleliu."

Eleven thousand Japanese were slain and more than two hundred captured. Most of the captured were forced laborers from Formosa and Korea. More than 1,200 Americans died and 6,100 were wounded. The 1st Division handed over Peleliu to the Army's 81st Division and returned to Pavuvu in mid-October. The land crabs and rats never looked so good.

POWS AND HELL SHIPS

A thousand miles west of Peleliu, dozens of Aggie POWs continued their dreary lives in the Philippines. It was now summer 1944 in the steaming POW camps—Cabanatuan, Bilibid, Santo Tomas, Los Banos, and Davao. For more than two years, the days had passed in squalor and hopelessness. The prisoners were slowly, but surely, starving. Those who survived into 1944 had their spirits buoyed a little by a decrease in the death rate and minuscule increases in water and food rations. Gardens were allowed by the Japanese at Cabanatuan, and the ingenious Americans invented all sorts of dishes—watery stews with snake weed and fish heads, baked goods using ground rice mixed with tooth powder, sauces using coconut oil and jungle herbs. Baked squash seeds became 'peanuts' and snake and cat meat made for 'steak.' Some even received Red Cross 'care packages' that were tearfully welcomed despite looting by the Japanese.

At Cabanatuan, Bill Porter got a package containing, among other items, corn meal. Like all the men, they had a desperate craving for baked goods. Porter traded his watch to a Japanese guard for two duck eggs, which he cracked open and poured into a canteen for hiding. Remembering something of his mother's baking on the family farm in the Mesilla Valley, he concocted a recipe for 'corn cake.' Carefully mixing the ingredients with the help of his drooling prison buddies, he popped the delicacy into a makeshift stove. As it baked, Porter and a growing horde hovered around inhaling the aroma, nearly mad with anticipation. Able to wait no longer, they took the steaming cake from the oven and gobbled it down. Many burned their mouths, but could not stop themselves. Though delicious, the cake was still wet inside. Porter and friends were soon doubled up and nauseous. Other POWs who received 'care packages' wolfed whole cans of meats and mouthfuls of crackers, cheeses, and jams. Several died from the shock to their ravaged digestive systems. Porter and his friends were lucky, they recovered.

All the POW camps were rife with rumor, some accurate, most just wishful thinking. Among the favorites were "We're gonna be exchanged for money and sent back home by Christmas," or "MacArthur will be back by late 1944." Hope, faith in God and country, and family memories were all they really had. At Cabanatuan, Christmas 1943, became a happening. The men decided to put on a big show. Clever skits, dances, and songs were rehearsed for weeks. Baked goods—rice cookies, squash bread and puddings were made. Even the Japanese guards and officers were invited to partake, and at least for a few joyous hours, brotherhood reigned.

As Christmas faded and spring led to summer 1944, the POW rumor mill was in high gear. In the depressing tedium of the camps, such talk was almost as welcome as food. But talk was cheap, and most rumors, especially the happy ones, had always proven false. But this time, the rumor was almost too delicious to contemplate. Word was out that MacArthur was on the move, that liberation was near! And this time, there was a difference. The POWs sensed a change in the Japanese guards. They seemed more docile, the officers not quite so prone to ravings. Then one day at Cabanatuan, several POWs saw "strange planes" in the sky. At the POW camp at Davao on Mindanao, Aggies Al Chase and Robert Remondini were electrified when they saw planes with an unmistakable marking—a big white star. Captain Russell Hutchison, 200th, of Albuquerque who was also confined at Davao confirmed the accuracy of the sightings. For weeks he had operated a crude radio receiver, cleverly concealed in a piece of hollowed mahogany. He received broadcasts about the American victories in New Guinea and the Central Pacific. He had to be careful, but he couldn't contain the news any longer. At long last, MacArthur was on the way back! Though emaciated and weak, the men felt exuberance for the first time in nearly three years.

Then fate dealt the POWs the cruelest of blows. The final horrifying saga of the 'hell ships' was about to begin. In a last ploy to use the POWs as a bargaining chip, the Japanese hurried to make ready their shipment from the Philippines to Japan before the onrushing American forces could capture the camps.

On June 6, 1944, the Japanese transport, *Yashu Maru* docked at Davao, loaded 1300 POWs and sailed for Manila. The Davao POWs were temporarily moved to Cabanatuan. On July 2, 1944, a thousand POWs, half from Cabanatuan and half from the recently arrived *Yashu Maru*, left for Japan on the *Canadian Inventor*. They endured a typhoon, close calls with American warplanes and submarines, but finally arrived in Japan on September 1, 1944. Several hundred died enroute due to disease and starvation.

Back on Mindanao, on August 20, 1944, Al Chase and Robert Remondini, along with 750 others were forced aboard an unidentified Japanese ship. It was the last POW group out of Mindanao. They docked at Zamboanga, where soon appeared the *Shinyo Maru* loaded with Japanese troops. That same night, the 750 POWs were hastily unloaded from the *Yashu Maru* under cover of darkness and forced aboard the *Shinyo Maru*, in effect, trading places with the Japanese troops. It was a gambit to fool the local guerilla intelligence network. Unfortunately, it worked very well.

On September 5, 1944, the *Shinyo Maru* headed north in convoy. Late on September 7th, the skipper of the U.S. submarine *Paddle*, thinking he was attacking a Japanese troop ship, intercepted and torpedoed the *Shinyo Maru* near Sindangan Point. Many POWs in the hold were literally blown apart. The Japanese locked the hatches and prepared to abandon ship. The surviving POWs made a human pyramid and were able to open the hatch and climb out. As they did, the Japanese shot many of them. Some made it to the water, only to be shot by other ships in the convoy. Of the original 750 on board, only 81 survived. Two brave, long-suffering Aggies, Albert Chase and Robert Remondini were not among the survivors who were rounded up again on the nearby beaches.

If only the pitiful survivors could have known what was going on elsewhere in the Pacific War, what a difference it would have made in their morale. For as they languished in confinement and as other Hell Ships plied the deadly waters, American forces were on a giant roll, smashing their way toward Tokyo. Kenney's aerial 'gangsters' had destroyed the Japanese air force in the Southwest Pacific, and Halsey's Navy and his brave flyers were now supreme (although the final, decisive Battle of Leyte Gulf still lay ahead). MacArthur's and Halsey's masterful campaigns in New Guinea and the Solomons had enveloped and isolated Rabaul where more than 100,000 Japanese troops sat frustrated and helpless, 'rotting on the vine.' And in the Central Pacific, Nimitiz's Naval, Marine, and Army forces had taken the Gilberts, Marshalls, Carolines, and Marianas under the command of Admiral Raymond Spruance.

By September 1944, MacArthur and Halsey had massive new staging bases at Hollandia in Northwest New Guinea and at Moratai less than 600 miles from the big southern Philippine Island of Mindanao. The table was now set for the invasion of the Philippines. Halsey's aviators got a close look at Mindanao, which had long been considered the first island for recapture. They met little Japanese resistance. And on Leyte, where there was a large force of Japanese troops, Halsey's planes encountered little challenge from the air. Halsey recommended to MacArthur that Mindanao be bypassed and Leyte invaded as soon as possible. Halsey suggested that the Leyte invasion be moved up to November 1944. Further planning moved it up to October. MacArthur was ecstatic.

As MacArthur's forces staged at Hollandia and Moratai for the invasion of Leyte, the now-panicked Japanese stepped up their insane orgy of 'hell ships' leaving the Philippines. On October 12, 1944, the *Arisan Maru* left Manila with 1,800 American POWs crammed in a hold big enough for less than half that number. The men began to suffocate almost immediately. The ship initially went south, then without explanation returned to Manila Bay on 20 October, the same day that U.S. forces landed at Leyte. In the week since they left, American planes had destroyed Japanese ships everywhere in Manila Harbor.

Even though a strong typhoon hit Manila on the 20th, the Japanese ordered the *Arisan* out. The POWs, ankle deep in feces and weak from dysentery and seasickness, went crazy in the darkness. The sane were forced to choke and kill some of those who had gone berserk in the desperately crowded hold. As the *Arisan* made its way north, it was torpedoed by an American submarine on October 24. Just as on the *Shinyo*, the Japanese sealed the hatch and tried to kill those attempting to get out. Hundreds died below or at the hands of the sadistic guards. As the *Arisan* took on water and began to list, the Japanese left on lifeboats or jumped overboard. They were soon picked up by other ships in the convoy. Many POWs in the water swam toward the same ships, but were met with gunfire or poked down with long bamboo poles. The hapless POWs retreated to the open sea, desperately clinging to boxes, boards, or anything else afloat. Scores drowned, but a few dozen hung on grimly. Back on the deck of the sinking *Arisan*, a group of POWs who could not swim sat together singing and praying. Soon the ship shuddered and slipped beneath the waves.

Among the dead in the *Arisan* disaster were Aggies Captain Hubert Jeffus, Private 1st Class Richard Hunt (Pinos Altos, '37), Sergeant George Jones (Lordsburg, '36), and Sergeant Arnold Orosco (Albuquerque, '39). All had been with the original contingent of New Mexicans of the 200th sent to the Philippines.

Of the 1,800 POWs who started the voyage on the *Arisan*, less than ten survived. One of the survivors was 200th veteran and New Mexican, Corporal Calvin Graef. He and another POW lashed poles and boxes together to form a raft and although delirious, hung on for a day. The next day, miraculously, they spotted and climbed aboard a lifeboat carrying three other POWs. Then more miracles occurred. The men spotted and picked up a wooden keg floating in the sea. It was filled with fresh water! Then they found a large box of Japanese food and a piece of canvas stashed in a compartment aboard the lifeboat. The men ate well before using the canvas to rig a sail and set for the China Coast 350 miles away.

Three days later they were picked up by a Chinese fishing boat and hidden. Onshore, the Chinese dressed Graef and the others as coolies and took them on an incredible journey through the everpresent Japanese. They moved hundreds of miles by foot, sedan chair, and truck to a new B-29 base under construction at Anlung. The construction techniques at Anlung had been at least partly developed by Captain John Silva (Clint, TX, '27) an ex-Aggie engineer who supervised construction of several other B-29 bases in China before his death in a plane crash in March 1944.

The Americans at Anlung were stunned to see Graef and the other emaciated POWs, whom they fed, fed some more, cleaned up and clothed. The POWs were first flown to Kunming for a debriefing by Halsey's staff. A few days later they took a long flight to the U.S. for more debriefings. It was then that Roosevelt and General Marshall first learned of the 'hell ship' incidents.

At the time of the *Arisan Maru* disaster, the destroyer *Lardner* was several hundred miles to the southeast patrolling off the recently captured island of Peleliu. The *Lardner*'s Captain had been warned about the treacherous coral reefs in the area, but most were poorly charted. As fate would have it, a twenty-year old Aggie Seaman, Jim Meadows, was at the helm. He had returned to the Pacific in spring 1944 from the U.S. after being reassigned from the carrier *Langley*. Suddenly, the *Lardner* ran aground on a reef and could not dislodge herself, even at high tide. A day later, a sea-going tug appeared and came along side. The tug pulled the destroyer off the reef, revealing a severely damaged bow. The *Lardner* was towed some 200 miles east to the huge new American installation at Ulithi Atoll.

Called by Admiral Nimitz, "the Navy's secret weapon," Ulithi was a massive complex for anchorage, resupply and repair of American ships. Located strategically near the island of Yap which was effectively isolated but still under Japanese control, Ulithi had been ingeniously transformed by Navy seabees. The atoll's thirty islets and surrounding reefs were developed into a first class shipyard and airstrip by November 1944. Nimitz enforced strict secrecy on combat reporters, although at this stage of the War and with the firepower on hand, the Japanese were believed unable to mount an effective attack on Ulithi. This was later proven false, as evidenced by a subsequent incident involving two Aggies—Navy flyers Jack Durio and future NMSU President Gerald Thomas.

Meadows' ship, the *Lardner*, arrived at Ulitihi and was put in dry dock where crack repairman immediately went to work on the damaged bow. For the next few days, Meadows and his shipmates indulged in the pleasures of the nearby islet of Mog Mog. King Ueg, local chieftain, had been previously persuaded to leave his royal digs on Mog Mog for another nearby islet. The Seabees quickly built a movie house, refreshment stands, a chapel, and other 'recreational diversions.' Men from the scores of anchored ships came to Mogmog in shifts to enjoy 'the four B's'—baseball, bathing, boxing, and beer. The beer was carefully rationed at two per man, but beer chits were gambled, bartered, stolen, or otherwise obtained by the more enterprising sailors to insure a pleasant buzz by late afternoon. Just before sundown, when the last ferry back to the anchored ships left Mogmog, the drunken 'gobs' were on the overcrowded ferry dock jockeying for position—shoving, fighting, and knocking one another into the water.

The officers had their own club on Mog Mog, and as befits rank, were allowed to buy fine bourbon and scotch at twenty cents a shot. They were permitted to fraternize with the only women allowed on Mogmog—Navy nurses. The nurses were expected to "avoid social encounters with enlisted men."

Jim Meadows and his shipmates had only a few days to partake of Mogmog because the *Lardner* was repaired in the unheard of time of three days. They were soon off to duty in the Philippines where the action on Leyte was well underway.

LEYTE —
AND THE AFTERMATH

MacArthur's long awaited return to the Philippines began at Leyte in October 1944. 'Bull' Halsey's naval air forces and George Kenney's flyers supported a massive, powerful invasion force of more than 700 ships and 174,000 troops. In *Reminiscences*, MacArthur painted a vivid picture of the Leyte landings.

> *The big guns ... opened fire at dawn. The noise, like rolling thunder, was all around us ... the blackness had given way to somber gray ... we saw the black outline of the shore on the horizon ... . And then, just as the sun rose ... there was Tacloban. It had changed little since I had known it forty-one years before on my first assignment after leaving West Point ... .*
>
> *Now thousands of guns were throwing their shells with a roar that was incessant and deafening. Rocket vapor trails crisscrossed the sky ... ugly pillars of smoke began to rise. High overhead swarms of airplanes darted into the maelstrom ... across what would ordinarily have been a glinting, untroubled blue sea, the black dots of landing craft churned toward the beaches.*

Aggie officers and men were in the thick of the action immediately. Ex-football tackle, Marine Sergeant Robert Shields (San Bernardino, CA, '39) was on duty with one of the landing ships off Leyte. Shields was hit by Japanese fire during the early period of the landing. He died from his wounds and was buried at sea on October 21st.

While Shields lay mortally wounded, the 96th Infantry Division with Lieutenant Colonel Jesse Mechem and Captain Wilber Fite landed near San Jose on the east coast of Leyte. With Mechem and Fite in the 96th were fellow Aggies Captain Carl Freeman and Captain

Henry Medinger. Some fourteen miles north of the 96th beachhead at San Jose, 1st Lieutenant Francis Gallagher and Major Jim Gerhart of the 1st Cavalry Division landed near Palo.

From the cruiser *Nashville,* just offshore from the 1st Cavalry beachhead, General Douglas MacArthur surveyed the scene through binoculars. The landings were going well. MacArthur had dreamed of this day since his humiliating escape from Corregidor three years earlier. As U.S. forces pushed inland, the joyous MacArthur could wait no longer. He ordered up a landing craft. With several of his generals, aids, newsmen, Colonel Carlos Romulo, and Philippine President Sergio Osmena, he made for the beach. The landing craft went aground in knee-high water fifty yards from shore. The Army beachmaster, "with hundreds of landing craft unloading and snipers' bullets spitting from the nearby groves," told MacArthur's party to walk. As the camera's rolled, the stage was set for MacArthur's dramatic "I have returned!" surf walk.

MacArthur met briefly on the beach with his onshore commanders, then strode proudly to a mobile Signal Corps radio microphone. His two-minute speech (some called it a sermon) was one of the most moving in the history of warfare.

> *This is the Voice of Freedom, General MacArthur speaking. People of the Philippines, I have returned! ... . By the grace of Almighty God our forces stand again on Philippines soil ... . The hour of your redemption is here. Your patriots have demonstrated an unswerving and resolute devotion to the principles of freedom ... . Rally to me! Let the indomitable spirit of Bataan and Corregidor lead on. As the lines of battle roll forward to bring you within the zone of operations, rise and strike ... . For future generations of your sons and daughters, strike! In the name of your sacred dead, strike! Let no heart be faint! Let every arm be steeled! The guidance of Divine God points the way. Follow in His name to the Holy Grail of righteous victory.*

Later that day, Gallagher and the 1st Cavalry fought inland against mounting resistance. Two days later, on October 22nd, they captured Tacloban and the adjacent airfield. On October 23rd an exhausted honor guard from the 1st Cavalry stood at attention as the Philippine and American flags were raised. An officer read a proclamation from President Roosevelt restoring the civil government of the Philippines. Tacloban would serve as the provisional capital until Manila could be recaptured.

South of the 1st Cavalry, the 96th Infantry and Lieutenant Colonel Mechem's 1st Battalion, 382nd Regiment were cutting a bloody swath through the Japanese. Over the next seven days, Mechem led his men on a steady advance toward the key town of Tabontabon, which fell on October 27th. On that same day, Wilber Fite was in action nearby as a company commander with another battalion of the 382nd Regiment. He was wounded by shell fragments. Mechem came to see Fite, wishing him well before his evacuation to New Guinea for hospitilization. Fite would remain hospitalized for three months before rejoining his unit after the Leyte campaign.

On October 29th after capturing Desahona, Mechem and the 1st Battalion swung eastward to join up with the 3rd Battalion. As they moved down the road to the east toward Kiling, eight Japanese appeared waving white flags. The Americans held their fire, honoring the apparent Japanese intention to surrender. Their act of mercy was repaid with treachery when the Japanese dropped the flags and took cover. The enemy opened up from all sides with machine guns and artillery hidden in the grass and nearby knolls. Mechem ordered the 1st Battalion to withdraw about 1,000 yards to a better defensive position. As they began the withdrawal, Mechem was hit and mortally wounded by machine gun fire. As he lay dying, his last order to his men was to fall back to defensive positions and not risk their lives getting his body out. Major Joseph Lewis, who took over the battalion, followed those orders initially. But after dark he led a small party forward and recovered Mechem's body.

By the next day, the battered Japanese had withdrawn. On a ridge near the site of Mechem's death, the men of the 1st Battalion erected a memorial to their fallen commander. The spot was officially named 'Mechem Ridge.' His men also dedicated a plaque to Mechem, signed by every man in the 1st Battalion. For his gallantry, Lieutenant Colonel Jesse Mechem was posthumously awarded the Silver Star. His death was another shock to the College and his friends and family in Las Cruces.

The Battle of Leyte raged for two more months. General Tomoyuki Yamashita's troops put up fanatical resistance. In desperation, the Japanese tried reinforcing their Leyte force by nighttime amphibious landings. Most of their troop ships and barges were annihilated with the loss of thousands of soldiers. They tried several ill-conceived parachute assaults on American controlled airstrips that ended in disaster. As the Japanese were cornered in northern Leyte, the fighting intensified. There, on November 13, 1944, Lieutenant Francis Gallagher was leading a company of men in an attempt to outflank a Japanese defensive line. Advancing with rifle and hand grenades, Gallagher had successfully blown several enemy pillboxes when he was cut down by Japanese fire. Gallagher died from his wounds that day, but according to his commanding officer, had been "an inspiration to all who witnessed his action." For his bravery, Gallagher was posthumously awarded the Silver Star. Tragedy had again struck a favorite son of Las Cruces and NM A&M.

By mid-December 1944, 'mopping up' operations were underway on Leyte. 'Mopping up' was a term MacArthur liked to use in press releases when he felt a battle was well in hand. It was a term hated by the troops left to do the 'mopping' because the Japanese would become even more ferocious when it became clear they were about to die. By the end of the Leyte struggle, the Japanese had more than 55,000 dead against only 2,900 Americans. Fewer than 400 Japanese surrendered.

Following the victory on Leyte, MacArthur moved his headquarters to the newly captured island of Mindoro just south of Luzon. Over the holiday period, MacArthur and staff worked around the clock refining plans for the invasion of Luzon and the capture of Manila and Corregidor. The fate of the POWs weighed heavily on MacArthur's mind, and with good reason. The POWs at Cabanatuan, Baguio, Bilibid, Santo Tomas, and Los Banos grew weaker by the day. But spirits soared as they witnessed squadrons of American warplanes overhead. These emaciated scarecrows-of-human-beings were having delicious sweet dreams, not of food, but of liberation. At Cabanatuan and in the other camps, clandestine radios broadcast news of Leyte and the imminent return of the Americans to Luzon.

But at Cabanatuan, the hopes and dreams of the long-suffering men were dashed again. In early December 1944, 1,619 American POWs were herded together and trucked to Manila. Incredibly, it was announced that they were being transported to Japan. The POWs were first in denial, then shock and anger. Bill Porter hurriedly penned a letter that he hid until liberated after the War

Dearest Folks:

I write this letter in great haste as I was just this moment informed that I will leave for Japan tomorrow morning at 5:30. I will not attempt to describe all the suffering, sickness, and hardships we have all endured. Nor will I lament at great length the misfortune of being snatched away from our redemption when it seemed so close … . If it means a thousand years, more blood and tears, I admonish you and the people of the United States that lasting retribution must be exacted. As for my family, in you I have found mental solace, hope, and strength. I pray with all my heart that you will love and understand one another and live in unity and prosper together … . I only hope that we can complete our trip safely so that we may be reunited once again. Failing in our reunion, I trust that you will receive this message and understand all those unsaid things that time and circumstances will not permit [me to describe] … . *In the next few lines, I will leave a simple will … .* [See pp. 151-52.]
Your loving son,
Bill

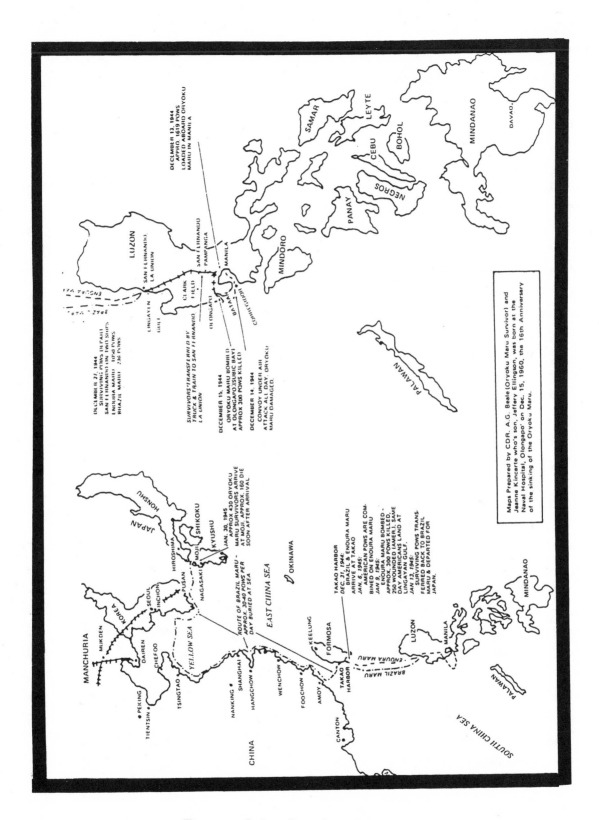

Route of the *Oryoku Maru*

On December 13th, the Cabanatuan prisoners, mostly officers, were loaded into the holds on the *Oryoku Maru* in Manila Bay. Bill Porter, and at least five other ex-Aggies including Captains J. Walter Donaldson (Deming, '37) and Gerald Greeman, were joined by more than a hundred other New Mexicans. The *Oryoku Maru* came under air attack by American planes on December 14th. There were more than a dozen POW casualties and several deaths from wounds and shock. But the ship was only lightly damaged and soon left for the next stop at Subic Bay on the west side of Bataan. A day later, as the *Oryoku* rounded Bataan near Olongapo, American warplanes struck again. This time 250 POWs were killed and the *Oryoku* severely damaged.

Gerald Greeman was one of the lucky ones. He made it to the deck and in the ensuing chaos charged the galley. He bolted down some rice and sardines, then found a dead Japanese and took his life jacket before going overboard. In the water, he joined scores of other POWs swimming toward shore. Some of the weaker drowned, and others were shot in the water by Japanese guards. Those that made shore, including Porter, Donaldson, and Greeman, were rounded up and marched to an old, wire-enclosed tennis court. There they were held like cattle on the blistering concrete for four days with virtually no food and little water.

But they gained hope as they witnessed repeated nearby bombing runs by American planes. Surely, now the Japanese would give up on the idea of shipping them off Luzon. Incredibly, they did not. Instead, the survivors of the *Oryoku Maru* bombing, less several dozen who died on the tennis court, were goaded onto trucks and taken to the railhead at San Fernando. Here they were given the 'boxcar treatment' again. Porter and his compadres wondered if it could get any worse. It could. Their Hell was only starting.

Transported to La Union on the Lingayen Gulf with yet another group of POWs, Porter, Greeman, Donaldson, and 1,050 other Americans were put on the *Enoura Maru*. Another 236 were loaded on the *Brazil Maru*. They embarked on December 27th. Conditions in the filthy holds were abominable, and this time, the sick, weakened men had bitter cold to combat. Many died of exposure or went insane. Some drank urine or bilge water and died. Scores succumbed of dysentery. Once a day the dead were flung overboard.

The ships arrived at Takao, Formosa, on December 31st where all surviving POWs were put on the *Enoura Maru*. While still in Formosa on January 9, 1945, the *Enoura* was bombed by American planes. Three hundred POWs were blown to pieces in the bombing. The next day, the dead were lifted off the ship in slings into barges manned by surviving POWs. The Japanese crane operators delighted in jiggling the slings. They thought it was funny to see the slimy, rotting corpses fall onto the hapless POWs in the barges below. The numb American prisoners rode the barges ashore, dug graves, and buried the bodies of their comrades.

On January 13th, the surviving POWs were moved back to the *Brazil Maru* for the final voyage to Japan. In bitter cold now, and with virtually no clothing, the pitiful POWs died at the rate of thirty-to-forty per day. The survivors finally arrived at Moji, Japan, on January 30th.

Aggie deaths during this the worst of all the Hell Ship tragedies, included Captain William 'Sleepy' Foster, and Private Francis 'Buster' Powell (Garfield, '39). Both were probably killed during the bombing at Subic on December 15. 1st Lieutenants Darwin Becker (Brenham, TX, '36) and Dallas Thorpe (Artesia, '37) died of exposure near, or shortly after, the end of the voyage.

But somehow, the indomitable Bill Porter had survived along with Walter Donaldson and Gerald Greeman. When the *Brazil Maru* finally made Moji, they helped lead the staggering, freezing, and starving Americans ashore. The Japanese doctors were aghast at their condition. The men were deloused and given dysentery inspections using a glass tube inserted up the rectum. Finally, they were given food, water, and clean clothing for the first time in more than a month. Some were even allowed to bathe.

Only 430 of the original 1,619 POWs who boarded the *Oryoku Maru* in Manila Bay had survived the horrible nightmare. Sadly, 160 of the 430 survivors of the voyage soon died of disease and exposure. The remaining 270 POWs' reward for living was yet another cruelty—another Japanese prison camp. Unbelievably, for Bill Porter, Walter Donaldson, and Gerald Greeman it got even worse. In a few weeks, they were shipped off to grey, cold Mukden, Manchuria, where they joined a number of American officers that included General Jonathan Wainwright, recently moved from internment in Formosa. Wainwright was later moved even deeper into Manchuria with a group of senior allied officer POWs.

DRIVE FOR MANILA

Instead of Mukden, imagine how Skinny Wainwright, Bill Porter, Gerald Greeman, and Walter Donaldson would have loved to be with their old commander General MacArthur, evening the score on Luzon. The mighty Luzon invasion fleet of 850 ships and 70,000 combat troops arrived at Lingayen Gulf, 110 miles north of Manila, on January 6, 1945. They had been subjected to vicious kamikaze attacks from the air and to sea attacks by 18-foot high-speed suicide boats filled with 500-pound charges. On the way to Luzon, a kamikaze dived into MacArthur's flagship, the cruiser *Nashville*, killing 137 hands. MacArthur was not aboard at the time. At Lingayen Gulf, a kamikaze plowed into the bridge of the battleship *New Mexico*, killing 32, including Winston Churchill's British Liaison officer, Lieutenant General Herbert Humsden. More than a dozen other ships were heavily damaged by the unrelenting kamikaze attacks.

MacArthur's plan was to land his 70,000 combat troops on the Lingayen Gulf beaches and drive across the plain to Manila. It was virtually a copy of the Japanese action four years earlier. There was no reason to be different. The earlier Japanese invasion and a 19th century American invasion had proven the Lingayen invasion strategy. To ensure that there would be no need to reenact Bataan in reverse, MacArthur's plan included landings by XI Corps near San Antonio on January 29th. Under Major General Charles Hall, XI Corps' mission was to take Subic Bay and seal off Bataan as an avenue of enemy retreat. They met fierce resistance at Zig Zag Pass, and it took nearly three weeks to complete their mission.

Under General Yamashita, the Japanese had 275,000 men on Luzon, but little air or naval support. Yamashita knew he couldn't stop the landing at Lingayen Gulf. He split his forces with the goal to inflict maximum casualties and delay on MacArthur. He sent 150,000 troops to the mountains of northern Luzon. Eighty thousand were dispatched to the hills east of Manila, and 30,000 took up fortified positions in the hills around Clark Field.

Yamashita, like MacArthur three years earlier, knew Manila could not be readily defended and planned to make it an 'open city.' Tragically, as it turned out, Yamashita was unable to control the 15,000 Japanese Navy troops that remained in Manila. Later, as the American entered Manila, these troops went on a horrifying, senseless orgy of murder, rape, fire, and pillage. MacArthur was furious, and after the final Japanese surrender in August 1945, went on a personal crusade to see Yamashita hang, which he did.

Following an intense barrage of the Lingayen beaches by the invasion fleet, the 6th Army under General Krueger came ashore on January 9, 1945. The 6th Army was organized into four combat divisions in two corps—XIV Corps under Lieutenant General Oscar Griswold (with Colonel Hugh Milton as his Chief of Staff), and the I Corps under Major General Innis Swift. General Swift's forces included the 43rd Infantry Division with ex-Aggies, Lieutenants Morris 'Pucker' Wood, Jack Horne, and Mark Radoslovich. Filipino guerillas had radioed from the Lingayen beaches that the Japanese were gone, and they were right. When the 70,000 men came ashore there was little resistance.

Within a few days, however, I Corps ran into heavy Japanese resistance on the east flank from Japanese entrenched in the hilly terrain. At first, XIV Corps had it easy. They drove steadily toward Manila. At each little town and barrio, Filipinos showered the troops with flowers, food, and drink. MacArthur quickly came forward by jeep, which was soon bedecked with flowers. Some said it resembled a Biblical-era chariot. War correspondents reported that "It was better than the Second Coming." And there was no mistaking that to the exuberant Filipinos, it was!

Off the Luzon landing beaches, the kamikazes continued their deadly attacks, and other Japanese planes based at Formosa had success bombing and strafing the American warships. On the carriers *USS Langley* and *Essex*, two pilots were carrying the air war to the Japanese bases on Formosa. One was former Aggie band member, Ensign Robert Hedley (Carlsbad, '40). The other was future NMSU President, Lieutenant (j.g.) Gerald Thomas. Both Thomas' and Hedley's squadrons were attacking Takao Harbor and Toshien Naval Base, Formosa. Despite withering antiaircraft fire, Thomas scored a direct hit on a Japanese destroyer at Toshien. For his action, Thomas received the Gold Star in lieu of a third Distinguished Flying Cross, the latter medals earned previously during more than fifty combat missions in Norway, China, Formosa, the Philippines, and Vietnam. He would later fly missions against Okinawa and mainland Japan.

On the same evening that Thomas returned to the *Essex*, Hedley returned safely to the *Langley*. He went immediately to the officer's stateroom to give a debriefing on his mission. Suddenly, a Japanese plane appeared and, despite blistering anti-aircraft fire, dove through the flak. It released a bomb that scored a direct hit just outside the stateroom. Hedley and dozens of others were killed instantly. He was buried at sea on January 22, 1945.

Back on the ground on Luzon, MacArthur fretted about the plight of the POWs at Cabanatuan and in the Santo Tomas, Bilibid, and Los Banos camps in Manila. He pushed General Krueger, who in turn urged General Griswold to move faster. But on January 23rd, Griswold's troops ran into advanced elements of Yamashita's 30,000-man force near Clark Field. A bloody weeklong battle ensued, resulting in the rout of the Japanese. More than

2,000 were killed, but the rest retreated deep into the mountains where they would hold out for months.

The one-week delay in moving toward Manila increased MacArthur's anxiety about the POWs. Finally, he and Generals Krueger and Griswold devised a bold plan. Elements of the 6th Ranger Battalion, supported by some 250 Filipino guerrillas, were sent silently through Japanese positions to the outskirts of Cabanatuan. There 500 American POWs awaited anxiously, unsure of their fate. The Rangers skilllfully cut the phone lines and on the evening of January 30, 1945 attacked the Japanese guards manning the towers and barbed wire at the camp. The Rangers were soon in control, but the numb, emaciated POWs were confused and scared. The Rangers prodded them to their feet and moved everyone out the front gate. Automatic weapons fire was heard to the south indicating that the guerillas had been engaged by an advancing Japanese force. The slow moving column of Rangers, guerrillas, and POWs staggered along through the night before arriving at the barrio of Sibul about 8 a.m. the next day. There a convoy of trucks and ambulances arrived to take away the grateful, but very weak POWs. The operation had cost the liberators one Ranger and 26 guerilas. The Japanese had lost 73 guards and 150 soldiers. The operation made headlines around the world, and MacArthur was at least partly relieved. But there was more work to do in liberating the POW camps.

Griswold ordered a group from the newly arrived 1st Cavalry Division to form two 'flying columns' of 700 men each and streak for the 3,800 prisoners at Santo Tomas. Major Jim Gerhart, executive officer of the 8th Regiment of the 1st Cavalry and *Life* photo journalist Carl Mydans rode in a jeep just behind the lead tanks. Griswold's 37th Division, and Colonel Hugh Milton, disappointed about not being the first combat troops into Manila after taking 100 miles of territory, would have to be content with following closely behind.

Under Brigadier General William Chase, the 1st Cavalry columns moved hell bent for Manila, so fast that they frequently got across bridges before the Japanese could blow them. As they closed in on Manila, they were forced to make more detours and river crossings. The columns were well supported by Sherman tanks and mobile 105mm howitzers, both of which were used effectively against the surprised, but dogged Japanese. Finally, on February 3rd, the 1st Cavalry reached the last river crossing at Novaliches, five miles from Manila. Amazingly, the bridge was still intact.

Jim Gerhart leaped from his jeep and ran up to Lieutenant Jim Sutton, a Navy bomb-disposal officer attached to the 1st Cavalry. "Come with me quick, the bridge is mined and the fuse is burning!" he shouted. Sutton raced onto the bridge with Japanese bullets zinging past him and cut the flaming fuse only minutes before it could blow the bridge sky-high.

As the armored column got ready to move out, Gerhart came running back to his jeep. Suddenly, he saw a Japanese some 75 yards away rise and begin running. According to Carl Mydans, Gerhart "without slowing his pace" and "with his carbine stock at his belly" fired and cut down the Japanese. He swung himself into the jeep, and the cavalrymen charged over the bridge past the dead and fleeing Japanese, firing from their vehicles as Gerhart had just done, 'John Wayne style.' When an excited Mydans commended him on his shooting, Gerhart replied, "Hell, I've been teaching my boys to shoot from the waist for three years. I sure had to show them I could do it myself." Gerhart told Mydans that he was organizer of the 'Revenge Bataan Unit' for the 'New Mexico boys' of the 200th Coast Artillery that had fought throughout Bataan.

As the 1st Cavalry column raced on, Mydans recalled "there was not a rifle or machine gun in the column which was not pointing outward, trigger fingered." They sped past several trucks of stunned Japanese on side streets, then past the Grace Park airfield on the edge of Manila where the hangers were on fire. As they entered northern Manila, jubilant Filipinos greeted them. Farther down Rizal Avenue, near the China University, they ran into a barricade and hostile Japanese fire. There, the two flying columns of the 1st Cavalry split, with Gerhart's group moving quickly toward Santo Tomas. The other column ran into an ambush and received heavy casualties.

Earlier that afternoon at Santo Tomas, a Marine plane dropped a small package inside the walled compound. An inmate retrieved the package, a pair of pilot's goggles wrapped in a note that read, "Roll out the barrel. Santa Claus is coming Sunday or Monday." As the electrifying news spread through the buildings and shacks of the old university, there was restrained jubilation. As it turned out, 'Santa Claus' came that very night.

Inside, 60-year old ex-Aggie John McFie and his wife Dorothy had been praying and hugging one another in anticipation of their liberation. They had been incarcerated for three long years. According to newspaper accounts summarized in the 'War Books,' it was on the night of February 3rd when an errant shell burst in the compound. John was struck by shrapnel and mortally wounded. He died a short time later. One can only imagine the emotions and trauma that Dorothy McFie must have experienced at that moment. (Published histories of the Battle for Manila suggest that the shelling of Santo Tomas was not intense until February 5th, continuing for several days. It may be that McFie was actually killed then rather than on February 3rd.)

The 1st Cavalry columns made the outskirts of Manila at dusk of February 3rd and pushed on against harassing fire from the Japanese. The columns were now strung out for forty miles, a dangerous circumstance that was never exploited by the shell-shocked Japanese. At 8:00 p.m. inmates at Santo Tomas heard shooting to the north. The shooting grew closer. Suddenly, Filipinos outside the gate were screaming "Mabubay! Mabubay!" (Hurrah! Hurrah!). There was a roar from the big Shermans, then a few minutes of silence followed by a booming American voice, "Where in hell is the goddamned front gate?"

Gerhart and several of his infantrymen went over the wall and engaged in a firefight and hand-to-hand combat with the Japanese guards. They located the front gate and partially opened it, before a Sherman tank labeled 'Battling Basic' crashed through. The remaining

Japanese guards flung grenades before retreating into one of the buildings. There they held several hundred women and children inmates as hostages. The 3,500 remaining inmates were unharmed, but could not celebrate until their comrades were freed.

The Japanese commander, Colonel Toshio Hayaski, ordered several Japanese to take two American hostages from the barricaded building and meet with the American cavalrymen in the main plaza of Santo Tomas. Lieutenants Luki and Kinoshita, with Lieutenant Abiko trailing, came forward to shouts of "Kill them! Kill them," from the throng of internees. Major Gerhart and his men relieved the Japanese of their swords and pistols, except for Abiko who refused to put up his hands. Instead, Abiko suddenly moved his hand into a pouch strapped to his shoulder. As recounted by Hartendorp in *The Santo Tomas Story*, as Abiko's hand went into the pouch, Gerhart grabbed a nearby soldier's carbine and shot the Japanese "without raising the gun to his shoulder." Abiko, groaning and writhing on the ground, was picked up and carried to the prison clinic. The internees, having endured years of Abiko's sadistic behavior, spat on him, slashed him with knives, and burned him with cigarettes as he came by. As Abiko was placed on a bed, the pouch on his shoulder fell open and a grenade rolled onto the floor. He died a short time later.

Gerhart's instinctive action had saved perhaps a dozen casualties. For his "extraordinary heroism" with the 1st Cavalry Division on Luzon, Jim Gerhart would receive the nation's second highest military honor, the Distinguished Service Cross. Colonel Roy Cole, who later taught at New Mexico Military Institute where Gerhart had finished a two-year degree before enrolling at NM A&M in 1938, stated that Gerhart was the most courageous, determined and unshakable combat leader he had ever seen.

The next morning, following Abiko's death, Lieutenant Colonel Charles Brady began negotiations with the barricaded Japanese commander, Colonel Hayashi. The bluffs, threats, and cajoling went on for hours. After a frustrating day of tense argument, Brady reluctantly worked out a deal. Hayashi and his sixty Japanese troops would be marched out of the compound under American guard to some point past 'American lines,' which in actuality, did not exist. Fighting was raging throughout Manila. The inmates were set free, and Brady was true to his word. The Japanese were escorted down the road a mile or so and told "You are on your own." For a moment, the Japanese balked thinking they were being double-crossed. The tense American cavalrymen fingered the triggers of their automatic weapons, but did not fire. The Japanese realized what was in store if they hesitated. Hayashi turned and formally saluted, then marched his column on without the Americans.

Now joined by a Battalion of the 37th Infantry Division under Colonel Lawrence White, the American troops at Santo Tomas had an opportunity to fully view the awful conditions. Life photographer Carl Mydans, himself an inmate at Santo Tomas until exchanged for Japanese newspapermen in spring 1942, made a series of heart rendering pictures. Filth and squalor were everywhere. Tattered clothes, bottles, and tin cans littered the floors. Many inmates, emotionally overcome and weak from starvation, could not speak. They tried but only gurgled. Terrified children hid behind their mothers. A wing of American survivors of Bataan and Corregidor was discovered. The men, hollow-eyed and skeleton-like, were a horrific sight. The liberating American soldiers wept at the scene.

The inmates desperately needed food and medicines. General Griswold dispatched a relief column under the command of Colonel Hugh Milton. Manila was still far from secure and Milton's unit was under small arms and mortar fire all the way to Santo Tomas. By this time, the Japanese had begun their atrocities against Filipino civilians. Milton and his men were enraged, and took no prisoners nor rendered mercy to the treacherous Japanese. They arrived at Santo Tomas on February 6th. Milton set up an operation to feed, clothe, and provide medical attention to the inmates. He then pushed on to Bilibid Prison located across town.

At Bilibid, Colonel Memory Cain of Deming, a 200th survivor of Bataan, was among the hundreds of military prisoners, of whom many were hospitalized and near death from disease and starvation. He recalled his encounter with Hugh Milton.

> *I was at Bilibid prison, down to 104 pounds when the Yanks came to liberate us. Suddenly, up front I heard somebody yelling, "Where's Memory Cain? Where's Memory Cain?" Hugh Milton showed up in battle dress and steel helmet. He sat and talked to me for about half an hour. Suddenly, he said "Memory, I'll be back. We're terribly busy today, and I'm behind on my quota." "Quota?" I asked, "What do you mean?" "I've assigned myself six Japs a day, and so far I'm at three," Milton replied.*

Later in the day, Milton returned to Bilibid, and Cain asked, "How'd you come out Hugh? Milton replied, "One over, got seven today."

For his gallantry in bringing relief to the prisoners at Santo Tomas and Bilibid prison, Milton was awarded the Silver Star. The commendation read

> *With the announcement of the liberation of the internees from Santo Tomas Internment Camp and Bilibid Prison, Colonel Milton proceeded to those locations to affect all possible relief and assistance. Passing through large areas that were not then occupied by our troops and under small arms and mortar fire, Colonel Milton reached his destination. Directing the procurement of supplies and remaining under fire to supervise their distribution, Colonel Milton was credited with a major role in saving the lives of the half-starved internees numbering nearly five thousand.*

As Milton's relief columns began pouring in supplies, MacArthur made his way into Manila and headed immediately for Santo Tomas. The grateful inmates, to whom his

118

presence was indeed a biblical happening, swarmed him. MacArthur was very moved. A short while later, MacArthur appeared at Bilibid to a wild welcome by the civilian internees. Aggie James Rice, recently moved to Bilibid from the prison at Baguio, was among those in the civilian group. But it was the reaction by the military prisoners at Bilibid that really moved MacArthur. It haunted him for the rest of his life. Author William Breuer described the scene in *Retaking the Philippines: America's Return to Corregidor and Bataan.*.

> *In the military section of Bilibid, in contrast to the turmoil in the civilian side, the supreme commander came upon lines of ragged soldiers— bearded, soiled, unkept, little more than skin and bones—each standing at attention by his cot, ready for inspection ... . A lump rose in Douglas MacArthur's throat and he fought back tears. These were his "boys"—the gaunt, grim, ghostly legion of Bataan and Corregidor.*
>
> *The eerie silence was broken only by the occasional sob of someone who could no longer fight back the tears. MacArthur passed slowly, down the lines of long-suffering men, through the debris of dirty tin cans they had eaten from, the bug-infested bottles they had drunk from. As he stopped before each filthy cot, a soldier would whisper weakly, "God bless you, General" or "Thank God you're back." His voice choked in emotion, MacArthur could only mumble, "I'm a little late, but we finally made it."*

Among the "gaunt legion" struggling to stand at his cot was Sergeant Tom Palmer. He was deathly sick and weak, racked with beriberi and severe malnutrition. But MacArthur's visit had inspired him, and he now looked forward to returning home to New Mexico. For the first time in months he gathered the strength to write to his parents in Albuquerque. The letter was in an almost illegible scrawl.

> *My hands in bad shape from beri-beri. This letter is incredibly tiring and I must stop frequently to rest ... . We can truthfully say we've come out of Hell into the Promised Land ... .*

Palmer thought back to that calamitous day at Clark Field three years before when the Japanese bombs fell on his New Mexico compadres. He remembered striding down the runway, trying to rally the troops, playing his trombone. ... *The old grey mare, she ain't what she used to be, ain't what she used to be ...* . He desperately needed to rest, and soon slumped back on his cot, shaking and utterly spent. A few days later, despite food, medicine, and the efforts of the newly arrived American doctors, his strength ebbed and his eyes closed. Sergeant Tom Palmer lapsed into unconsciousness and died. It was February 13, 1945.

THE 'ROCK'

The fighting raged on in Manila, now street-by-street, building-by-building. The defenders were revengeful Japanese Naval troops under Rear Admiral Sanji Iwabuchi. Iwabuchi had disregarded General Yamashita's direct orders to make Manila an open city. His troops were now laying waste to the once beautiful Capitol City—slaughtering Filipino civilians, raping the women, bayonetting babies, and summarily executing the men after tying their hands behind their backs.

Just outside Manila, the Japanese made suicidal stands in defensive positions at Fort McKinley and Nichols Field. As usual, pillboxes had to be taken one by one with grenades and tanks firing point blank. Even then, Japanese would appear unexpectedly through a back door, charging with a rifle and bayonet.

Finally, American firepower and doggedness began to turn the battle. As the rout began, the Japanese retreated with hundreds of Filipino hostages into the beautiful old walled portion of Manila known as Intramuros. The walls were tens of feet thick, and there were numerous courtyards, alcoves and fortified windows from which the Japanese took cover and returned fire. General Griswold installed loudspeakers and pleaded with the Japanese to surrender, telling them that the situation was hopeless and that they would be well treated. The Japanese declined. After forbidding aerial bombardment in deference to the Filipino hostages and civilians, MacArthur reluctantly gave permission to shell Intramuros. The smoke, dust and noise from the awesome bombardment were stupefying. But the Japanese sailors held on, refusing to yield or surrender.

As Manila was burned and blasted, MacArthur pushed on to the next major objective—the capture of Corregidor, the sacred 'Rock.' Corregidor, the symbol of MacArthur's humiliation and despair, was now the symbol of his redemption. But it was also vitally important to the military. Manila Harbor was of little use unless Corregidor was in American hands.

The capture of Corregidor was undertaken as a combined sea-air-land operation. The primary forces would be the 503rd Parachute Infantry Regiment (now at Mindoro), and the 3rd Battalion, 34th Infantry Regiment of the 24th Infantry Division. The Japanese commander on The Rock was Navy Captain Akira Itagaki. American intelligence estimated that Captain Itagaki had only eight hundred troops. He actually had more than 5,000, outnumbering the initial American attack force by two to one. They were dug in at Malinta Tunnel and hundreds of other caves and tunnels all over Corregidor. They had huge stores of ammunition and other supplies. And like the situation at Lingayen Gulf, Itagaki had a small flotilla of high-speed suicide boats to deter American warships. But he had reccurring nightmares about an airborne assault on Corregidor by the Americans. His superiors scoffed at the idea as impossible—the landing zone on the 'Topside' portion of the island was too small, they assured Itagaki.

Early on the morning of February 16, 1945, more than 1,500 503rd paratroopers 'mounted up' on Mindoro and loaded onto dozens of C-47s for the flight to Corregidor. Each man was laden with sixty to one hundred pounds of gear—weapons, ammunition, life preserver, pack, and parachute. A 22-knot wind played havoc with the drop, which was made from only a few hundred feet above the ground on Topside. The men hit the treacherous ground after only one or two oscillations of their chutes. It was bone jarring, and there were dozens of broken ankles and legs. At first Japanese resistance was light. The bombardment had kept them in the caves.

Twenty-five men of I Company targeted to land on the old golf course, instead drifted hundreds of yards southeast over Breakwater Point. They landed two hundred feet above the water on the edge of a cliff. They got out of their chutes and scrambled back along a trail toward the golf course. As they rounded a bend in the trail, they saw Japanese standing looking off toward Geary Point where the 3rd Battalion, 34th Infantry was landing. The paratroopers deployed and opened fire with automatic weapons and grenades. The startled Japanese returned fire, but were soon overwhelmed. Almost unbelievably, among the dead Japanese was Captain Itagaki. His top aide was captured alive. Itagaki had been at the main Japanese observation post and was so entranced by the amphibious landing and deafened by noise that he and his men had not even noticed the 503rd's airborne assault. The loss of Itagaki severely hindered the Japanese efforts to coordinate the defense of Corregidor. But as always, the Japanese proved to be extremely tough and fanatically brave.

Rooting the Japanese from the amazing cave and tunnel complex was excruciating. Many tunnels were so deep and well ventilated that standard flamethrower tactics, so effective on Peleliu and other Pacific islands, were of little use. But the Americans quickly learned what did work. Soldiers raked the cave entrance with automatic weapons to force the

Japanese deeper inside, out of return-fire range. Then an unlighted stream of jellied fuel was squirted in. Finally, depending on the size of the cave, a white phosphorus grenade or satchel charge would be thrown in. Thus, the caves were systematically destroyed and its occupants buried, burned alive, or blown to pieces. There was no choice. The Japanese would not surrender.

The enemy crept out of the tunnels at night in large numbers, and climbed up the cliffs or crawled between shell holes toward the American foxholes. On several occasions, they overran American positions and killed dozens of surprised, exhausted soldiers. But in the process, hundreds of Japanese were slaughtered.

By the end of the first week, there were more than a thousand rotting Japanese corpses on the island. The smell was nauseating, but it wasn't half as bad as the flies. Millions of the voracious insects swarmed in dense black clouds. In desperation, the Army Air Corps sent C-47s over to spray the island with an oil-based DDT mist. While today's EPA would not have approved, the American soldiers were deeply grateful. The fly problem was brought under control immediately.

The Japanese defenders conceived a last ditch plan. On February 21st, all was silent as night fell. As recounted by E.M. Flanagan in *Corregidor, The Rock Force Assault*, at 11:30 p.m. "Corregidor rolled like a ship at sea, [and] the Bataan Peninsula reverberated and trembled, so great was the explosion. Flames poured from all the tunnel entrances ... ."

Huge boulders were thrown into the air, and landslides thundered downhill to the shore-line. As the dust settled, fifty Japanese marched out the west entrance of Malinta Tunnel "as if on parade." The infantry squad guarding the entrance was at first dumbfounded and permitted the Japanese to move about fifty yards into the open. But suspecting the usual treachery from the Japanese, the Americans "opened up with everything, cutting them down like grain." Soon, more Japanese came out in ones and twos, and they too were cut down. Later it was learned that the detonation was intentional, but that it had gotten out of hand and detonated a huge store of munitions. It was another example of senseless banzai tactics gone awry.

On March 1st, after more brutal cave-by-cave battles and many Japanese suicides, The Rock was officially declared secure. On that day Colonel Jones directed the 503rd unit commanders to police the parade ground at Topside. Tomorrow there would be a big day. Jones had received word that General Douglas MacArthur was returning to The Rock.

At 10:00 a.m., on March 2, 1945, a proud Supreme Commander landed at Corregidor in a PT boat at South Dock. With the stench of Japanese corpses in the air and smoke billowing from several tunnels above, MacArthur rode in a jeep caravan to the east entrance of Malinta Tunnel. He went inside to where he and Skinny Wainwright had endured the fearful Japanese bombardments three years earlier. He next went to view some of the gun emplacements at Wheeler Battery. Finally, the jeeps wound their way to 'Topside' and stopped at the parade grounds. It was 11:00 a.m. and the skies were bright. A slight wind was blowing off Manila Bay.

MacArthur, hesitated a few seconds, then in an emotional voice said,

> *Colonel Jones, the capture of Corregidor is one of the most brilliant operations in military history. Outnumbered two to one, your command by its unfaltering courage, its invincible determination, and its professional skill overcame all obstacles and annihilated the enemy. I have cited to the order of the day all units involved, and I take great pride in awarding you as their commander the Distinguished Service Cross as a symbol of the fortitude, the devotion, and the bravery with which you have fought. I see the old flagpole still stands. Have your troops hoist the colors to its peak, and let no enemy ever haul them down.*

As buglers sounded "To the Colors," the flag was raised with MacArthur watching intently. MacArthur awarded the Presidential Unit Citation to the entire 'Rock Force.'

A few minutes later, as MacArthur's PT boat left South Dock, a Japanese sniper was killed near Malinta Tunnel. Over the next two weeks, more than a hundred more Japanese were rooted out of the tunnels and killed. Nine months later, on New Year's Day, 1946, a sergeant with a graves registration company was at the command post when he looked up and was startled to see a formation of twenty Japanese marching toward him. Dressed in fresh uniforms, they were waving surrender flags. Their leader explained that a newspaper had blown into their cave telling of the Japanese surrender.

When it was all over on Corregidor, nearly 6,000 Japanese were dead. American deaths numbered nearly three hundred with 1,000 wounded.

IPO AND LOS BANOS

Coincident with the battles for Corregidor and Manila, Aggie soldiers were fighting on Luzon with the 43rd Infantry Division. After the initial landing at Lingayen, Lieutenants Pucker Wood, Mark Radoslovich, and Jack Horne served to support a series of actions to dislodge Japanese troops from the mountainous terrain on either side of the Lingayen plains north of Manila. These battles, always against determined, virtually suicidal Japanese resistance, would go on for nearly eight months, into August 1945.

In one key operation, Jack Horne's 118th Combat Engineer Battalion, 169th Infantry Regiment, 43rd Division was given the job of securing Metropolitan Road leading to Ipo Dam in the Sierra Madres east of Manila. Ipo formed one of the main water supply reservoirs for the capital city. Horne's company had bull dozers and heavy equipment that was working to clear tons of rock that had been blasted onto the road from the shelling of the Japanese dug in along the Bigti Palisades above. As Horne's battalion worked up the road, tanks were brought up to attack the Japanese. But the tankers balked at going further, fearing land mines. Seeing the situation, and at great personal risk, Horne jumped on the front of a dozer and rode part way up the road under small arms fire from the Japanese above. The road was eventually cleared by the dozers and TNT demolition, opening the way for the tanks and infantry to attack and neutralize the Japanese and secure Ipo Reservoir. For his actions at Ipo, Jack Horne was awarded the Silver Star.

As the 43rd battled north and east of Manila, the last of the big Luzon Japanese prison camps, Los Banos, was still in Japanese hands. On the grounds of the former Philippines Agricultural College, Los Banos Prison housed more than two thousand malnourished inmates, mostly civilians who had been in Manila when it fell in early 1942. They included nuns, priests, missionaries, doctors, engineers, businessmen, and more than two hundred wives and children. Among the captives was Martha Trogstad, wife of William Trogstad, who had died two years earlier as a POW at Cabanatuan. Another prisoner was George Gray, brother of ex-Aggie Lieutenant Edward Gray of the Navy, who at that moment was with the invasion fleet off the coast of Luzon. George, legal counsel to the American High Commissioner Francis B. Sayre, had been incarcerated at Santo Tomas before being moved to Los Banos in 1943 with a large group of civilian internees.

At Los Banos, as at Santo Tomas, Gray was a leader in organizing the inmates and negotiating with the Japanese for better living conditions. Soon after arriving at Los Banos, Gray was elected secretary of the POW 'camp committee.' Gray and the committee had a good intelligence system and were aware of the American landing at Lingayen in January. At the risk of his life, Gray made several daring nighttime forays through the camp barbed wire to meet with local Filipino guerilla leaders. Reporting back to the committee, Gray passed on the electrifying news that a rescue attempt was in the works. The committee members grew timid and decided that further contact with the guerrillas was too dangerous, that the POWs were better off doing nothing so as not to tip off the Japanese. Gray heartily disagreed, and secretly took his own action to ensure that if a rescue attempt came, it would be well coordinated. Failure would almost certainly result in the slaughter of the entire camp.

Gray and several others continued to sneak from camp at night for meetings with the guerrillas. They provided valuable documents and hand drawn maps of Los Banos and other information on Japanese strengths and weaknesses, habits of the guards, etc.

As recounted by William Breuer in *Retaking the Philippines*, it was a Sunday morning in February 1945, and American Sister Patricia Callan was walking to the crude chapel at Los Banos where one of the sixty-five Catholic priests with enough strength to stand was to preside over the mass. Sister Patricia noticed drums of gasoline, new machine gun emplacements on the hill above the camp, and a large, freshly dug trench just outside the barbed wire. After the War it was learned what the Japanese guards had been ordered to do in the event the Americans approached Los Banos. They were to pour the gasoline on the inmates' straw huts and other structures and set them ablaze. As the inmates ran to escape the flames they were to be cut down with the machine guns. Then there would be a mass burial in the trench.

Despite the success of the Luzon operations so far, MacArthur had good reason to worry about Los Banos. He ordered General Joseph Swing, Commander of the 11th Airborne Division to liberate Los Banos "as soon as you can." Swing was left to figure out how. He knew it was not going to be easy. Besides the camp guards, there were 8,000 men of the Japanese 8th Division located less than ten miles away. Then there was the huge lake, Laguna de Bay, that bounded Los Banos to the north, blocking much of the land access to Manila.

During the planning stages of the rescue operation, a civilian escapee from Los Banos dispatched by George Gray found his way to General Swing. He was an engineer named

Peter Miles, and he was able to draw precise maps of the compound. He noted that only the on-duty guards at the camp were armed. The remaining arms were locked in an armory on the grounds. Miles told General Swing that all the guards took daily calisthenics together just after sunrise in an open area near the barracks, a few hundred yards from the armory. With the detailed new intelligence, General Swing and his staff developed a cunning, if risky, plan based on split-second timing and surprise.

Liberation day was set for Friday, February 23rd. First, a unit of thirty men would paddle across Laguna de Bay at night in native canoes and slip ashore at Mayondon Point, two miles north of Los Banos. There they would join up with a Filipino guerrilla force that had been watching the camp from the hills. Armed with Tommy guns and grenades, this 'killer platoon' was to creep undetected to the guard posts and wait for a signal to attack, exactly at 7:00 a.m. Their job was to kill all the on-duty guards.

Simultaneous with the 'killer platoon's attack, a company of paratroopers would bail out of nine C-47s and land next to the camp. Once on the ground, the airborne troops would race the off-duty guards to the armory to prevent them from arming themselves. Meanwhile, another group of paratroops would be on their way across Laguna de Bay in fifty-four amtracs, having left Mamatid at 4:00 a.m. The amphibious craft were scheduled to land at Mayondon Point precisely at 7:00 a.m., just as the other actions occurred. These craft would be used to ferry more than 2,100 inmates to safety across the lake, but it would require two trips to take everyone.

Finally, to keep the Japanese 8th Army Division pinned down in their positions along the San Juan River, a diversionary attack would be mounted south along the highway from Manila. It was intended to make the 8th Division deploy and delay any response to the Los Banos operation for several hours.

At 7:00 a.m. on February 23, 1944, "all hell broke loose" at Los Banos. William Breuer described the action.

> *Lieutenant Skau and his Killer Platoon pounced on the Japanese guards, gunning them down and hurling grenades. Confused and panicked, guards surviving the first assault ran around aimlessly until they too were cut down ... . Meanwhile, Lieutenant Ringler's parachutists had made an almost text-book-perfect landing ... . Ringler's men rushed the barbed-wire fence and were soon inside. Startled by the sudden assault from the blue, the Nipponese off-duty guards milled about in confusion, then, sizing up the situation, dashed for the structure holding their weapons. It was too late: Ringler's jackrabbits had already won the race.*

Sister Patricia ... had reached the chapel ... . Inside the ramshackle structure the sister and others flung themselves face-down onto the dirt floor. The Catholics among them began reciting the rosary out loud ... . As Sister Patricia Marie poked her head through the open window to look skyward, bullets began ripping through the thin walls. The Maryknoll nun flopped to her floor, but periodically got to her feet and went to the window to give those stretched out flat a play-by-play account of the action ... . "For God's sake," shouted a Jesuit priest who had taken refuge under a makeshift altar, "get down, Sister, get down" ... . His pleas were followed by more grenade detonations.

Suddenly, an American paratrooper carrying a Tommy gun rushed through the door.... To these servants of God who had never seen an American soldier in combat gear, with steel helmet, jump boots, and baggy pants, this warrior seemed like Superman ... "Where are the Japs?" the lanky paratrooper called out. "There's none in here," a shaky voice responded. The American turned and dashed back out the door ... .

Meanwhile the fifty-four amtracs were on their way inland from Mayondon Point. The lead amtrac reached Los Banos and crashed through the front gate. Inside, the prisoners were a chaotic mob, some jumping for joy, others cowering in their shacks too afraid to come out. The only thing the operation's planners had forgotten was now sorely needed—a bullhorn to give the scattered, confused inmates some reassurance and instructions. Fires were breaking out all over Los Banos, and as smoke billowed, the inmates came out of hiding and began moving toward the amtracs. Paratroopers ran into the camp hospital and carried out a hundred and thirty patients. They found several fresh corpses that were wrapped in blankets and carried to the amtracs.

Jammed with internees, the clattering amtracs finally made for Laguna de Bay. The remaining internees walked under guard to the shore of the lake where to await their turn to ride to safety across the waters. As one amtrac loaded with nuns rumbled by the mile-long column of soldiers and liberated prisoners, laughter erupted. In huge letters on the side of the vehicle was its name: *The Impatient Virgin*.

As the internees waited on the lakeshore for the return of the amtracs, mortar shells began falling in the area; then machine gunfire. Elements of the Japanese 8th Division were on their way to Mayondon Point. Anxious minutes passed as the terrified inmates huddled together. But soon, the churning amtracs appeared on the lake, heading back. There were loud cheers. Twelve hundred inmates and soldiers were loaded aboard and ferried across the lake. General Oscar Griswold, Commander of IV Corps, was waiting for them at Mamatid on the other side. The 11th Airborne Division had already been known as the 'Angels from Heaven.' It seemed a perfect moniker to the grateful inmates who had just been saved by the paratroopers. In actuality, the name resulted from the 11th's reputation for pilfering supplies from quartermaster stores throughout the Pacific. When confronted the paratroopers would smirk and innocently look skyward as if they knew nothing.

All 2,147 internees and more than 400 soldiers survived the daring rescue. The lone casualty was a woman inmate who had been nicked by a rifle bullet. Martha Trogstad, George Gray, and the other liberated prisoners were taken north to Manila for housing, food, and medical attention at the Bilibid Prison farms. Colonel Hugh Milton had arranged for air drops of supplies for the liberated civilians. They would be well taken care of and soon they would be going home.

Manila fell in March, but the 43rd Infantry Division and other elements of MacArthur's ground forces continued 'mopping up' the stubborn Japanese on Luzon well into the summer of 1945. On the other Philippine Islands to the south, new battles raged as American forces landed. The fight for Mindano and nearby islets was especially tough. In one battle on Cebu Island, Lieutenant Wade H. Corn, Jr. (Roswell, '43), of the Americal Division was killed. He was posthumously awarded the Silver Star.

CHINA

USSR

HOKKAIDO

Vladivostok

Tumen R.

SEA

OF

JAPAN

Yalu R.
Chosan
Changjin
Sinuiju
Chongchon R.
Unsan
Hamhung
Hungnam
Wonsan
Pyongyang
Kumchon
NORTH
KOREA
Panmunjom

38°
38

Kimpo
Seoul
Chunchon
Wolmi Do
Wonju
Inchon
Suwon
SOUTH
KOREA
Osan
Han R.
Yongdok
Taejon
Kunsan
Taegu
Naktong R.
Pusan

Sendai

HONSHU

Nikko
JAPAN
Tokyo
Kawaguchi
Yokohama
Kamakura
Nagoya
Atsugi
Hayama
Kyoto
Sagami Bay
Kobe
Nara
IZU
Hiroshima
Osaka
IS.
MIYAKE

Korea Strait

TSU
IS.

Inland Sea

SHIKOKU

MYOJIN

Sasebo

Bungo Strait

CHEJU

Nagasaki
Kagoshima
KYUSHU

SUMISU

EAST

TORI

CHINA

30

TANEGA
YAKU

SOFU GAN

30

SEA

AMAMI

JAPAN
and
KOREA

TOKUNO

NISHINO

BONIN IS.

IE

OKINAWA

0   100   500
Kilometers

RYUKYU IS.

0   100   500
Statute Miles

VOLCANO IS.

IWO
JIMA

130

140

IWO JIMA, ULITHI, AND OKINAWA

As the battles continued in the Philippines, a number of Aggies were 1,500 miles to the northeast on a small, sulfur-stenched volcanic island in the Pacific. There, on Iwo Jima, one of the most famous battles of the Pacific War was taking shape. Like Peleliu, some doubted the need for taking Iwo Jima. Bristling with more than 25,000 dug in Japanese defenders on high ground overlooking the landing beaches, Iwo was obviously going to be costly. But in the midst of an all out B-29 bombing campaign of the Japanese mainland launched from U.S. airfields in the Mariana Islands 800 miles to the south, Iwo was important for several reasons. First, because it was adjacent to the long flight path to the mainland, the Japanese on the island were providing early air raid warnings to the mainland. Second, as the battered B-29s returned from the Japanese mainland, many were forced to ditch in the Pacific before reaching the Marianas. The B-29s desperately needed an emergency landing field as well as a base for fighter escorts (new long-range Mustangs) to accompany them to Japan. Taking Iwo Jima would solve all these problems.

The Japanese commander on Iwo Jima was Lieutenant General Tadamichi Kuribayashi. As a Captain in the late 20s, he had taken cavalry training at Fort Bliss. He was aware of the hopelessness of a successful defense of the island, but was determined to kill as many Americans as possible. His strategy was straight out of Peleliu. Kuribayashi built an incredible, interconnected series of reinforced caves, bunkers and pillboxes on Mt. Suribachi and other high points. This provided pre-zeroed in fields of fire aimed at the landing beaches. To conserve manpower and maximize the effectiveness of his fire, Kuribayashi ordered that his ground troops not fight on the beaches nor engage in banzai charges.

Preceded by an awesome naval and air bombardment, American Marines of the 3rd, 4th, and 5th Divisions swarmed ashore on hundreds of landing craft. Overhead Navy pilot Lieutenant Jack Durio, flying off the 'new *Lexington*' in his Curtiss 'Hell Diver,' was among the screaming planes of Air Group 9, bombing and strafing the Japanese. Also in the air was another Aggie, Marine Captain Warren Wright (Portales, '40), a forward air observer. On the ground were other Aggie Marines, grimly battling up the soft volcanic beaches, fighting yard by yard through withering Japanese artillery, machine gun and mortar fire.

Iwo was hell on earth for more than four weeks. When the brutal nightmare ended on March 25, 1945, the 25,000-man Japanese force had been annihilated, but at great cost. More than 4,200 Americans were killed and nearly 20,000 wounded. Among the dead were at least three Aggies—Captain Warren Wright, Corporal Robert M. Ortiz (El Paso, '41?), and Corporal William A. Eakens (Las Cruces, '42). Ortiz, an infantryman with the 4th Marine Division was posthumously awarded the Navy Cross for killing fifty Japanese with a flamethrower and saving the lives of a cave demolition team.

Lieutenant Jack Durio lived to fight another day. In early March he was reassigned from the *Lexington* and ordered to report to the carrier *Yorktown* at the fleet anchorage at Ulithi. There, unbeknownst to Durio, he would be joined by future NMSU President Gerald Thomas.

After flying missions against the Japanese on Formosa and Okinawa, Lieutenant (j.g.) Gerald Thomas and the carrier *Essex* headed for Ulithi Lagoon on March 2, 1945. There, Thomas received amazing, happy news. He and his Torpedo Squadron Four were being sent home. Few flyers deserved it more. He had logged more than 1,000 flight hours and made ninety carrier landings.

At Ulithi, Thomas was given the job of inventorying the equipment and personnel gear that the replacement squadron would be inheriting from his Torpedo Squadron Four. He was disappointed in not being able to fully brief the new flyers about the latest tactics and tricks the Japanese were using at the time on Okinawa, Formosa, and the Japanese main islands. He had recently seen several comrades die from concealed anti-aircraft fire from 'dummy airfields' that were used to lure in the American planes.

Shortly after he transferred to the *USS Long Island* in Ulithi Lagoon for the trip to Pearl Harbor, the Japanese paid a farewell visit recounted in Thomas's journal.

> *Torpedo Four was finally headed for stateside—after three tours of duty; one in the Atlantic on the* **Ranger** *with the British Home Fleet; one on the* **Bunker Hill** *in the Pacific (starting with strikes on the Philippines); and a third on the* **Essex** *(ending with the invasion of Okinawa). Now we were in Ulithi Lagoon, transferred to the baby flattop* **Long Island** *for the trip back home.*

It was after dark. Makibbin and I were up on the flight deck watching the crew load damaged planes for the trip back. The flight deck was lit up like a Christmas tree ... the war was nearly over (perhaps) ... Ulithi was ... a long, long way from the Japs—except for Yap Island ... .

*... Mak and I were talking about the trip home when we heard planes overhead—two, at least. [They] sounded different from any we were used to ... so we speculated out loud on the kind of plane. Both of us finally decided the strange sound was probably the new Curtiss float plane ... . About the time we reached this conclusion, there was a huge explosion on the **Randolph** anchored next to us. Fire followed the explosion. Mak and I immediately ran around the flight deck of the **Long Island** trying to kick out the lights— anything to prevent a further attack by what obviously was a kamikaze.*

When the kamikaze hit the *Randolph*, Jack Durio was watching a movie below deck on the *Yorktown*, a short distance away. A few minutes later, as everyone raced for the deck, Durio heard another explosion. Gerald Thomas on the *Long Island* actually saw the source of the second explosion. Another kamikaze had dived into Mog Mog, apparently mistaking the islet and its lights for an aircraft carrier. Fortunately, for the thousands of men frequenting Mogmog, the massive liquor and beer stores were not destroyed. But damage on the *Randolph* was heavy. Fires and explosions followed. The men worked frantically to control the damage. Four hours later, at midnight the flames were finally extinguished. But twenty-five men had been killed and 106 wounded.

Later that night, the smoky voice of Tokyo Rose was heard on the ship's radio. She announced that the attack had been prearranged to ruin Jack Durio's evening on the *Yorktown*. "Think you're nice and safe at Ulithi don't you? Well, we're fixing a little surprise for *Yorktown*."

Later it was learned that the kamikazes were 'Frances' twin-engine bombers sent all the way from Minami Daito Shima, 800 miles north of Ulithi. Only two of the inexperienced pilots found Ulithi. The wreckage of the one that hit the *Randolph* revealed that the pilot had been shackled to his cockpit.

After the kamikaze incident, Thomas and his squadron left Ulithi on the *Long Island* and made Pearl Harbor on March 23, 1945, and then San Diego on April Fools Day, 1945. Ironically, it was also Easter Sunday. On that day, Jack Durio and the *Yorktown* were readying for battle, as were Major Henry Gustafson; Captains Wilber Fite, Henry Medinger, Carl Freeman, and Roy Skipworth; and Lieutenant Ed Gray. They were among dozens of Aggies poised to fight the last great battle of the Pacific War—Okinawa.

*　　*　　*

Okinawa, a dreary island of 700 square miles, was the next American target on the drive to the Japanese main islands some 350 miles to the north. Okinawa was an ideal staging area for the massive American build up that would be needed to mount the invasion of Japan. The island had wonderful harbors, airfields, and both flat and hilly terrain for troop training. Consequently, bypassing Okinawa was not an option. However, MacArthur later criticized the Navy command for not bypassing the southern portion of Okinawa after the early initial successes in taking the rest of the island.

With the fall of the Philippines and Iwo Jima, Japanese defenses had been so constricted that a vicious, concentrated defense was expected on the Okinawan landing beaches. Japanese commander, General Mitsuru Ushijima had a formidable force at his disposal—more than 100,000 men, hundreds of tanks and artillery pieces, and 3,000 aircraft. And the terrifying kamikaze menace, refined by the lessons of Leyte, Luzon, and Iwo Jima, was expected to be worse than ever.

At 8:00 a.m. on April 1st, a huge landing force of two Marine and two Army divisions loaded into amtracs for transport to the main landing beaches near Hagushi on the lower western coast of Okinawa. Unexpectedly, it was deathly quiet!

At first, the nervous men thought of April Fools Day. But then, viewing the pastoral scene on the peaceful beaches, it was obviously more like Easter. Marine 1st Lieutenant David Brown wrote of the "furrowed fields of ripe white winter barley, and tiny bright field flowers ... scattered over the light earth. We were all incredulous, as if we had stepped into a fairy tale."

What nobody realized was that General Ushijima had conceded the Haushi landing area, and virtually all of the northern two thirds of Okinawa. He had moved his 100,000 men into deeply fortified positions to the south along natural east-west ridgelines and cliffs that bisected the narrow island.

Fite, Medinger, and Freeman with the 96th Division and Roy Skipworth with the 7th Division landed on the first day and moved south. Gustafson, commanding the 3rd Batallion, 5th Regiment of the 1st Marine Division also landed on April Fools Day. In his words,

> *Experiencing no enemy fire on the beach, I moved as rapidly as possible, making every effort to maintain contact with my executive officer. After moving my command post about 2 miles inland, I was talking on the SCR radio when a sniper shot me. The bullet shatterd a bone in my left arm and put me out of action. I could not believe that I became the first casualty in the regiment and had to relinquish my command to my executive officer and be evacuated.*

New Mexico journalist Ernie Pyle, fresh from the European theatre, had landed with the Marines and came to visit Gustafson. Pyle's next column described the light casualties and said that "a major had been wounded." Back in the States, Gustafson's sister Evelyn suspected, correctly, that Henry was the major in question.

Gustafson was evacuated to the big military hospital on Guam where he underwent surgery and two weeks of recuperation. While there, three Aggies heard of Gustafson's presence and paid a surprise visit. They were Lieutenant (j.g.) Cecil Pickett (?, '40), U.S. Navy, 1st Lieutenant Michael Taylor, U.S. Marines, and Lt. Colonel James 'Whiz' Bradford, (?, '39), U.S. Army. Taylor was in the Guam hospital himself, a victim of dengue fever. Gustafson was soon transferred to Hawaii, then back to San Diego for recuperation. For him, the Pacific War was finally over.

Meanwhile on Okinawa, American forces moved ahead under sporatic resistance, capturing airfields, towns, and communication centers and befriending thousands of Okinawans on the way. It had all seemed like a big, but very strange party. The GIs and Marines grew more nervous by the day. Was April Fool's still in store?

1st Lieutenant Roy 'Bud' Skipworth of the 7th Division and Captain Wilber Fite of the 96th Division soon found out. Skipworth, while advancing southward with the 84th Infantry Regiment, was cut down and killed by enemy fire on April 5th. His parents and loved ones in Portales drew scant consolation from the posthumous Purple Heart, or from the Silver Star earned earlier by Skipworth during the fight for Kwajalein.

The next day, on April 6th, 700 Japanese aircraft and 350 kamikazes attacked the American ships and landing beaches on Okinawa. In a final desperate act, the Japanese committed their last great battleship, the *Yamato*, along with eight destroyers and the cruiser, *Yahagi*. Dispatched from Japan, the Japanese fleet had no air cover. The *Yamato* had only enough fuel for a one-way trip. At 72,800 tons, she was the heaviest ship afloat and sported nine 18-inch guns that could fire a 3,200 pound shell twenty-two miles. For defense, she had radio jamming equipment, 100 antiaircraft guns, and armor plating that was up to 16 inches thick. Flying off the *Yorktown*, Lieutenant Jack Durio and his mates with Squadron VB 9 were among a group of divebombers ordered to attack the *Yamato* task force. Durio's mission was the cruiser *Yahagi*. Durio and several others of his squadron scored direct hits. The cruiser was sent to the bottom.

Following their attack, Durio and his Squadron VB 9 circled and watched as Navy torpedo bombers struck the crippled *Yamato* relentlessly. As the torpedoes struck home, the *Yamato* began smoking and listing. In a matter of minutes, the massive battlewagon rolled on her side and slipped beneath the waves with thousands of Japanese sailors still aboard. In less than two hours the *Yamato*, *Yahagi*, and four of eight Japanese destroyers were gone. The Imperial Fleet had vanished.

For his heroic action, Durio was awarded the Navy Cross to go along with many other decorations received in the Pacific, including two Distinguished Flying Crosses (one for bombing Tokyo).

Back on Okinawa, Wilber Fite had been grazed on the head by a Japanese sniper bullet, but recovered quickly and soon returned to action leading his K Company of the 382nd Regiment. On April 14th, during a furious artillery and infantry battle with the Japanese, Fite was struck by shrapnel. The metal pierced his helmet and entered the brain. Carried to a field hospital, Fite underwent crude surgery before being evacuated to Guam and, finally, to Tripler Hospital in Honolulu. Fite would endure years of recuperation before living a normal life again. But he was out of the Pacific War, and would receive a much-deserved Silver Star.

A day after Fite was wounded, on April 15th, Ernie Pyle went ashore with the Army's 77th Division on the islet of Ie Shema off the main island of Okinawa. A bloody 6-day battle ensued against the Japanese who were entrenched on a small volcanic cone that dominated the island. The engagement cost more than 1,150 American lives before the Japanese were wiped out. One of the American dead, victim of a sniper bullet to the head, was New Mexican, Ernie Pyle. The American GIs on Ie Shima erected a simple marker that Pyle would have appreciated. It read: "On this spot the 77th Infantry Division lost a buddy, Ernie Pyle." The news saddened New Mexico and all of America.

Pyle's body was later buried with thousands of American troops in the hauntingly beautiful 'Punch Bowl' cemetery overlooking Honolulu.

Although the land battle for Okinawa was mean and bloody, the naval action and kamikaze attacks were just as desperate. American sailors endured thousands of the screaming, banshee-like actions. Many suffered combat fatigue and nervous breakdowns due to the never-ending harassment. Every day, from mid-April until early June, the skies around Okinawa were alive with tracer rounds and diving Japanese planes whose pilots were relentless in their determination to kill and die for the Emperor. Aggie Jim Meadows, aboard the destroyer *Lardner* on screening duty, was witness to the kamikaze fury. In all, by the end of the Okinawa campaign, more than 1,400 kamikaze flyers were killed. But more than 7,000 American sailors were wounded and 4,300 killed, and hundreds of American ships were badly damaged. Forty were sunk.

Fortunately, Jim Meadows and the *Lardner* went relatively unscathed. But that didn't stop Tokyo Rose from reporting the *Lardner*, and many other American ships, as sunk by the "magnificent warriors of the Divine Wind." These 'sunk' U.S. vessels became what Admiral Halsey called the 'ghost fleet'—a fleet that would pay a revengeful visit to the Japanese in Tokyo Bay a few months later.

In May 1945, Aggie Lieutenant Edward E. Gray (brother of George Gray, recently liberated from Los Banos Prison in the Philippines) was aboard the destroyer *Longshaw* off the southwestern Okinawa coast. Gray was gunnery officer on the gutsy little ship that had fired more than 8,000 rounds on Japanese land positions and repelled dozens of kamikaze attacks. On the morning of May 18th, the *Longshaw* was beginning shore bombardment operations when it suddenly went aground on an uncharted reef off the coast near Naha. Unable to free herself despite the best efforts of the Captain and crew, the *Longshaw* soon came under fire from Japanese shore guns. Gray rushed to the forward magazine and directed return fire, but the shells from the Japanese artillery were deadly accurate. Six shells hit the forward magazine and blew up the entire front section of the ship. The director, with Gray inside, was knocked off its tracks, and dangled part way overboard. Inside, Ed Gray lay bleeding and mortally wounded. He never regained consciousness, and died the next day. It was a devastating blow to his mother on the family farm in La Mesa, and to his brother George who had miraculously survived more than three years of incarceration on the Philippines. Ed Gray's posthumous Bronze Star was little consolation.

Back on Okinawan soil, Carl Freeman and Henry Medinger 'rode out the storm' with the 96th Division to the bitter end. At the height of one thunderous battle, American and Japanese guns went strangely silent. Suddenly, everyone knew why. An American scout dog and an Okinawan cur of the opposite sex approached each other from opposing lines. They eyed one another, liked what they saw, and quickly 'got down to business.' Loud cheers erupted from the Japanese and American sides as the love struck dogs finished their debauchery and trotted back to their defensive positions. The shooting then recommenced, as furious as ever. The incident became affectionately known as the 'Truce of the Fucking Dogs.'

Into late May, the out-manned Japanese put up a wild, suicidal defense in southern Okinawa. With guns and soldiers dug deeply into the low ridgelines overlooking the approaching Americans, they spewed a deadly curtain of fire. Carl Freeman was among thousands of American soldiers wounded by shrapnel from the barrages. Fortunately for Freeman, his Purple Heart did not involve a lost limb or serious injury. Henry Medinger, Freeman's Aggie classmate with the 96th Division's Combat Engineers was also wounded, but not seriously. Besides the Purple Heart, Medinger's actions on Okinawa led to his award of the Bronze Star.

Finally, in tactics that had become all too familiar to the GIs and Marines, the Japanese were dispatched from their caves and pillboxes with 'corkscrew and blow-torch' tactics— blazing streams of fire from flamethrowers, grenades and satchel charges. It was agonizing, horrifying work. Thousands of Japanese were slaughtered without mercy, because they would accept none.

When it was finally over on Okinawa more than 110,000 Japanese and 12,000 Americans had been killed. The land battle essentially ended on June 22, 1945 when General Ushijima and his subordinate, General Cho, knelt before their headquarters cave on Kunishi Ridge and committed hara-kiri.

The immediate thoughts of the American troops now turned to caring for the thousands of pitiful Okinawan civilians. Elsewhere, at headquarters throughout the Pacific and in Washington, plans were being developed for the invasion of Japan. In the Philippines and other allied-occupied islands, and on the ships, every GI, Marine, airman, and seaman dreaded the idea. MacArthur, feverishly planning the invasion, told President Truman to expect one million American casualties.

Meanwhile, under the command of General Curtis Lemay, American B-29s rained explosives and firebombs on the major Japanese cities. Tokyo was especially hard hit. Hundreds of thousands of Japanese civilians perished under the punishing bombardment. Japanese radar and anti-aircraft fire were not effective against the high flying B-29s, but with enough warning, specially equipped Zeros could make just enough altitude to challenge the 'B-sans.' They employed kamikaze tactics, and in many cases were effective in ramming the American bombers. During one of the big B-29 raids, Aggie James Toliver (Vaughn, '41) was killed over Tokyo in February 1945. His body was never recovered. Another Aggie airman, Lieutenant Robert L. Carr (Tularosa, '42) met a similar fate on July 9, 1945.

THE A-BOMB

From their prison camps in Japan, the Allied POWs witnessed the effectiveness of the B-29 raids. At Yokohama, Niigata, Hirohata, Kosaka, and Tsuruga, New Mexican POWs were among those cheering as their barracks were hit and damaged. Some were beaten for their display of emotion, but to them, it was well worth it. The Japanese were on the run and being punished in their own homeland.

Returning from work detail in Yokohama in July, Winston Shillito saw virtually nothing in the city left standing. Tokyo had been firebombed almost into oblivion, as had other major Japanese cities and industrial centers. But ex-Aggie John Farley, a medical officer with the 200th and now a POW at Nagasaki on the southern Japanese Island of Kyushu, thought the skies too quiet. He knew of the bombings on the main island of Honshu, and a few Kyushuan cities had also been hit. Why was there no bombing at Nagasaki?

President Harry Truman stepped up the pressure on the Japanese. Surrender or be destroyed, he threatened. But to the Japanese, surrender was still unthinkable, and the B-29 raids continued, killing thousands of civilians each week.

In July 1945, the 43rd Infantry Division was headquartered at the former Japanese POW camp at Cabanatuan, nervously awaiting orders. Jack Horne, 'Pucker' Wood, Mark Radoslovich, and the others knew they were slated for the invasion of Japan. They had practiced amphibious landings and conducted mock land battles. They had stayed in shape—calisthenics, marches, obstacle courses, baseball, and touch football. The waiting was no fun, but at least they had good food, beer, and a little nightlife from time to time.

In Las Cruces several Aggies had come home from the war on leave—Jack Durio, Tom Esterbrook, Mert Gillis.

Early on the morning of July 16, 1945, a few Las Cruceans saw a bright flash over the nearby Organ Mountains, then a dull roar. The Army put out the word that an ammunition dump had exploded at White Sands. But it was no ammunition dump.

Conceived in the secret labs of Los Alamos under the direction of the brilliant physicist Dr. Robert Oppenheimer, the atomic bomb would change the future of mankind. Oppenheimer stood transfixed by the blinding flash and huge fireball that burst on the cool New Mexico desert that morning. He was reported to have recited two passages from the Hindu epic, *Bhagavad-Gita*. The first was, "If the radiance of a thousand suns were to burst into the sky, that would be the splendor of the Mighty One." The second: "I am become Death, the shatterer of worlds."

On August 6th, Jack Horne and his 43rd buddies were watching a movie at Cabanatuan when the word came. A new secret weapon had been unleashed on Hiroshima, devastating the city. The bomb had been dropped from a B-29, the *Enola Gay*, flying from its base in the Marianas at Tinian. Was this the beginning of the end? Everybody prayed it was so.

Three days later on August 9th, John Farley was in the POW camp at Nagasaki.

I was looking toward the Mitsubishi plants five miles from camp when I saw a terrific flash. The light was projected upward as well as downward and quivered for thirty seconds. I hit the ground ... I heard breaking glass ... I saw a tall white cloud-like pillar four to five thousand feet high. Inside, it was brown and churning.

For the next week, dentist Farley helped tend to the sick and dying. Forty-eight POWs and many guards had been killed by the mighty blast. Nagasaki had ceased to exist—100,000 perished within seconds and thousands more would sicken and die agonizingly slow deaths over the coming months, victims of hideous burns and radiation poisoning.

The following day, August 10th, the Japanese 'sued for peace,' contingent upon certain conditions, including one that Hirohito be retained as Emperor. After careful consideration, Truman and the Allies reluctantly agreed. On August 15th, Emperor Hirohito went on radio to tell his devastated subjects that all was lost, that they would have "to endure the unendurable."

The word of peace was slow in coming to the POW camps, but when it did, the men went wild with glee. All across Japan, American supply planes and bombers flew low over the camps, now well marked with white 'POW' letters on roof tops. They dropped canned meats, peaches, catsup, bread, cigarettes, magazines, and whiskey! Some of the POWs were injured and a few killed trying to 'catch' 55-gallon drums falling from the sky. The men gorged themselves, threw up, and ate again. Many went over the wall and marauded in the surrounding towns—a dangerous undertaking considering that American troops were not yet ashore to keep order. Some jumped on Japanese trains, to the astonishment of civilians, and rode to Tokyo or Kobe in search of Americans.

At the POW camp at Fukuoka #3, Major Winifred Dorris of the 200th, accepted the sword of Camp Commandant Yaichi Rikitaki and offered him the opportunity that Rikitaki had endlessly given Dorris over the last year—"as a coward for having chosen surrender, it is now your duty to commit suicide." Rikitaki declined the honor to the smirks of the assembled American POWs.

News of the Japanese defeat came especially slowly to the big POW camp at Mukden, Manchuria. Bill Porter and the other POWs had heard distant rumblings, which they later learned were the sounds of the approaching Russian Army fighting the Japanese. On August 16th, the POWs saw six men bail out of a "strange plane" near camp. They were an American OSS team sent to secure the safety of the POWs before rescue missions could be mounted into Korea and Manchuria. The OSS men were stripped and surrounded by angry Japanese and forced to kneel. Major James Hennessy, leader of the OSS group, told the Japanese the war was over. They were led to Camp Commandant, Colonel Matsuda, who contacted Tokyo. Matsuda got the grim news; the Emperor had ordered surrender. The camp quitting bell was wrung, and the announcement made. **"WAR OVER."**

Three days later, American planes landed with food, music, and a speaker system. The POWs put the speakers on the parade ground and played "Sentimental Journey" over and over again. Shortly, a "wild-eyed, rag-tag bunch" of Russians arrived. Bill Porter sized them up quickly and remarked to his buddies that given the opportunity, the Russians would be worse than the Japanese. For awhile, everyone got along. Mukden was declared an open city. The POWs marauded, drank vodka, commandeered the local brewery, and gorged themselves on food. Meanwhile, the Russians were busy pillaging, drinking, and raping. Soon they turned sullen toward the Americans. American supply planes had their tires slashed, then were ordered not to land at all. Finally, the Americans were ordered out. The POWs thought it was a blessing. Among those leaving were a group of the happiest Aggies in the world—Bill Porter, Walter Donaldson (very sick), Gerald Greeman, William Coleman (Hot Springs, '36?), 200th, Andrew 'Jiggs' Robinson (Hillsboro, '38?), 200th, Ernest Armijo (Los Lunas, '32?), 200th, and Charles 'Dick' Nunn (Hillsboro, '38?), 200th.

To the north, at another Manchurian POW camp full of high-ranking American officers, the long-suffering General Skinny Wainwright, was evacuated and flown on toward Manila, and then Tokyo for a meeting with MacArthur. To all, General and Private, Admiral and Seaman, freedom was the sweetest thing of all!

Bill Porter was in heaven. He wrote home once again.

Mukden, Manchukuo
August 19, 1945
Dear Folks:

   This isn't going to be much of a letter; what's the use of trying to narrate all that's happened in four years when you are so surprised, elated, and confused that everything is hazy. It all came about rather spectacularly here. A plane dropped six men near here in parachutes ... [to] supervise our transition. Their arrival was supposedly pre-arranged, but our local Japs didn't expect them—didn't even know the war was over! Quite some excitement for awhile!

   Well, the turnover has been very easy—much easier than expected. We don't know how we will leave here, or just when, but I'll be home soon I'm sure. We left the Philippines on Dec. 14 '44 after the American attack had begun and were sunk the morning of the second day. Our second ship was bombed and disabled in Formosa, but our third ship made it. Ray Bliss and Jerome Triola were left in the Philippines. I hope they come out all right ... [at this point, Porter's letter was censored] *... sweated, starved, and tortured us, so I don't guess they've been* [concerned] *about mail. Personally, I think I'm in fair condition at present, but won't know for sure until I undergo a medical exam. In the past I was very ill and may have a few hangovers. I have many plans; but all lie far ahead. As yet the near future is too fast changing ... . The very thought of our reunion sends me into ecstasy, and when we are all together again, nothing, absolutely nothing, will ever separate us again like this. I've had too much time to work things out in my mind—there is nothing in this world of importance at all except a man's family, and just a few chosen friends. You'll understand this better after we've talked a while.*

   Well folks, a lot of these guys are trying to cram three pages full of hardships, gripes, dangers, glories, and starvation. They really are letting their hair down—that's all a lot of foolishness. The only thing important and worthwhile writing is that I am free, well, and we are all to be together soon ... . As opportunity arises, I will keep you posted on what they plan to do with us. Oh, before I close—please contact Mrs. [censored] *... I'll contact her myself when I come home. We'll, I'll close now—all I do is eat-eat-eat—the first I've had of plenty since Dec. 8, '41.*

God bless you all—we'll soon be together. My love to Grandaddy, Ernest, Gloria and all the family.

Your affectionate son,
Bill

As the POWs made their way from Manchuria toward the Philippines or Okinawa for medical attention and processing for shipment to the U.S., American warships and sailors were converging on Tokyo Bay. Jim Meadows on the *Lardner* was among them. The *Lardner* and scores of other American ships now formed the "ghost fleet," those ships reported sunk by Tokyo Rose and Japanese propagandists. The savvier of the Japanese citizenry saw first hand how grievous had been the lies of the Japanese war machine. The Japanese were thunderstruck before the mighty armada of American and British ships assembled in Tokyo Bay. "How did we ever think we could defeat such a power?" many asked themselves quietly. It was a good question.

On September 2, 1945, only a few thousand yards from the battleship *Missouri*, Meadows and his *Lardner* crewmates watched entranced as General Douglas MacArthur, with General Wainwright and British General Arthur Percival immediately behind him, presided over the formal surrender ceremonies.

Also anchored in Tokyo Harbor was the attack cargoship, *USS Libra* with Aggie C. Quentin Ford (Glenwood, '49) aboard. Ford, who had started school at NMA&M in 1941, spent one and a half years at the Merchant Marine Academy where he received a Navy commission in 1944. Assigned to the *Libra*, Ford saw duty during landings at Bouganville, Iwo Jima, Leyte and Luzon. In Tokyo Bay on the momentous day, the *Libra* had brought the radio station from Manila by which the surrender ceremony would be broadcast worldwide.

The deck and railings of the *Missouri* were overflowing with American sailors and brass of every service and every ally—British, Dutch, Australian, New Zealand, and Russian. A master of high drama, MacArthur made a brief, magnanimous speech, prayed for an end to war, and closed the ceremonies in less than twenty minutes. He treated the Japanese dignitaries with great courtesy, much to the annoyance of several American admirals and generals who wanted them humiliated.

After the surrender ceremony, MacArthur beamed a broadcast to the American people.

Today the guns are silent. A great tragedy has ended. A great victory has been won. The skies no longer rain death—the seas bear only commerce—men everywhere walk upright in the sunlight. The entire world is quietly at peace. The bold mission has been completed. And in reporting this to you, the people, I speak for the thousands of silent lips, forever stilled among the jungles and the beaches and in the deep waters of the Pacific which marked the way. I speak for the unnamed brave millions homeward bound to take up the challenge of that future which they did so much to salvage from the brink of disaster ... .

And so, my fellow countrymen, today I report to you that your sons and daughters have served you well and faithfully with the calm, deliberate, determined fighting spirit of the American soldier and sailor, based upon a tradition of historical truth as against the fanaticism of an enemy supported only by mythological fiction. Their spiritual strength and power has brought us through to victory. They are homeward bound—take care of them.

The *Lardner*, which had earlier been involved in transporting POWs (and gorging them with gallons of ice cream) from their camps in Japan to American staging areas near Tokyo, was selected for a new mission. With the battleships *Tennessee* and *California*, a tanker, and her sister ship the *Landsdown*, the *Lardner*, with Torpedoman Jim Meadows aboard, was ordered to make an around the world goodwill tour before returning to New York. They were to go by way of South Africa and South America. The South American part of the trip was cancelled, however, due to political unrest in Brazil. Meadows and his shipmates didn't care since it only meant getting back to New York earlier than anticipated. They sailed into New York Harbor and the beautiful sight of the Statue of Liberty.

In Manila, New Mexican POWs clustered at the 29th Replacement Depot, the gathering center for the return trip to the U.S. There, many of the men saw each other again for the first time in years. There were bear hugs and tears of joy. Then as the men calmed down and asked questions of one another, there were tears of sadness for the many friends who had not made it. The seriously ill, like Walter Donaldson, were quickly evacuated by air. The others ate, then ate some more, played cards, and partied in Manila while awaiting word of their transport ships.

Gerald Greeman was told to stand by for 'air alert' and to pack no more than fifty-five pounds of baggage. He didn't know what was up, but was soon informed that he was among eighty POWs that had been named a 'Hero of Bataan.' Greeman, along with fourteen other New Mexicans, was selected as a ceremonial detail for a big celebration in Honolulu. He arrived by air on September 20th for the festivities and parade. Five days later, Greeman and many of the other 'Heroes' flew over the Golden Gate and landed at Hamilton Field outside San Francisco. His wife was there for a jubilant reunion.

Like many of the other returning POWs, Bill Porter was severely underweight and racked with tropical parasites. And there were other troubles. On the way from Manchuria to Manila, his transport ship was engulfed by a typhoon, then hit a mine. The ship had to be towed to Okinawa for repairs. That didn't stop the irrepressible Porter from having fun. Okinawa and the next port, Manila, had plenty of booze and other distractions. And the card games were wild. Porter was a shrewd poker player and did well on the slow voyage to San Francisco. Winnie Porter Price (Las Cruces, '41) was on the dock in early November when Porter's ship came in.

> We were scanning the boat with field glasses, but the men on deck just looked like a football game crowd. I heard someone yell Winifred, and there was Bill waving a $500 bill .... The boys had played poker all the way home.

Porter's parents were with Winnie, and the reunion was wonderful. But they were shocked to see Bill's condition. He was little more than "skin and bones." But Porter's toughness and positive attitude carried him through. He and several shipmates were taken to Letterman Hospital in San Francisco for rest, observation, testing, and treatment. In two weeks, he had gathered strength and was out of the hospital for the ride home to El Paso.

Many of the other returning Aggies and New Mexicans came home via train from the West Coast. As they came into the state, many got off at the first station and kissed the cool desert ground. Those who were still ill and wounded were sent for recuperation to the Bruns General Hospital in Santa Fe. Santa Feans treated them like royalty—it was almost impossible for a veteran to pay for a meal or a drink. It was the same all over New Mexico—her sons were lavished with kisses, favors and celebrations.

WAR'S END

The POWs and other veterans were finally coming home. But some Aggies, most notably a few in the 43rd Infantry Division and 1st Cavalry Divisions and newly promoted General Hugh Milton, still had work to do. They made a landing on the main island of Japan and became part of the occupying force. Milton was put in charge of a large administrative staff in support of the provisional Japanese government under the overall command of General MacArthur. The Americans had expected trouble—there were still hard line Japanese militarists around and a dissident kamikaze group. But things went smoothly. The Japanese people accepted their fate as vanquished, and under MacArthur's enlightened direction, the reconstruction of a nation's infrastructure and psyche moved ahead quickly.

By fall 1945, General Hugh Milton made the decision to come home and resume his duties as President of New Mexico A&M. Milton's wife, 'Jo' and two young sons, John and Hugh, III, had been without him since September 1941. His school and family were overjoyed to have him back.

At a Board of Regents meeting on December 1, 1945, it was decided that General Milton would resume his duties as President as of January 1, 1946. The Board, at Milton's urging, also made plans to honor Aggie veterans and General Jonathan Wainwright in Las Cruces on the occasion of his countrywide tour scheduled to pass through Deming and El Paso in less than two weeks. Everywhere he went, crowds went wild at the sight of the scarecrow-like Wainwright. He was the emotional symbol of American perseverance against a brutal enemy.

At Deming, Wainwright paid tribute to the brave New Mexican's of the 200th. Following the 200th ceremonies on December 12th, Milton led an entourage to Deming to escort General Wainwright to Las Cruces. Governor Dempsey, Colonel C.G. Sage, Deming, Commander of the 200th, and several other dignitaries joined Milton in a police-escorted motorcade. Las Cruces closed all businesses and celebrated as the famous General made his way down Main Street and then to campus. There, at Williams Gym, he was joined by an overflow crowd of 3,000 that included twenty-three Aggie POWs, other Aggie veterans, and a group of Gold Star mothers—mothers who had lost their sons in the War.

Following an organ processional by Edith Porter, the crowd sang the national anthem, and the Reverend Hunter Lewis, a mainstay on campus for decades, gave the invocation. Governor Dempsey made a brief speech and acting President Branson presented Wainwright with an honorary Doctor of Laws degree. Wainwright then made a humble acceptance speech, insisting that his honors be bestowed "not so much upon me personally, but upon the brave men and women it was my privilege to lead in a forlorn hope." He then turned dead serious with a plea for national readiness; not to make the mistake of taking our freedom and armed forces for granted. He expressed confidence that "A&M college, having made such a tremendous manpower contribution to the war effort, would continue to do its share and more to help preserve peace."

As he ended his speech, Wainwright thanked the men and women who had supported him in those dark days in the Philippines four years earlier. As he sat down to the cheers and heartfelt love of the audience, the old cavalryman flashed back to that ghastly scene of May 1942 below Malinta Tunnel. He remembered his favorite poem ...

Fiddler's Green

Halfway down the trail to Hell
In a shady meadow green
Are the souls of all dead troopers camped
By a good old time canteen,
And their eternal resting place
Is known as Fiddler's Green

Marching down straight to Hell
The Infantry are seen
Accompanied by the Engineers
Artillery and Marine
For none but the souls of Cavalrymen
Dismount at Fiddler's Green.

Some go curving down the trail
To seek a warmer scene
But no Cavalryman ever gets to Hell
Ere he's emptied his canteen.
And so rides back to drink again
With friends at Fiddler's Green.

And so when a horse and man go down
Beneath a saber keen
Or in a roaring charge or fierce melee
You stop a bullet clean
And the hostiles come to get your scalp
Just empty your canteen
And put your pistol to your head
And go to Fiddler's Green.

The printed program for the ceremony included a passage honoring Aggie veterans.

In honoring a great soldier this afternoon, New Mexico A&M is also symbolically paying tribute to the 2,113 men and women from this college who served in the late war—to the 103* who lost their lives, to the many who are still missing, to those who languished in hospital and prison camp. One-fifth of its former students followed the colors in all theaters of the war. From the beginnings on Bataan and Corregidor—where they fought beside today's honored guest—through Anzio and Normandy to the final conquests of Berlin and Tokyo, wherever there was action there were men and women of A&M. Many of them are here today. Many others are absent forever. The presence of you, the living, the absence of the departed, imbues your Alma Mater with the determination to perpetuate your indomitable spirit—the spirit that sustains and bespeaks America.

The POWs in the audience thought of their comrades and buddies who had suffered and died at the hands of the Japanese. They recalled the 'POW oath' and vowed to remember …

---

* More than 125 dead have now been identified. See Appendix C.

They shall grow not old, as we that are left grow old, Age shall not weary them, nor the years condemn; At the going down of the sun, and in the morning, We will remember them ... .

As the crowd filed out of Williams Gym into the late afternoon shadows, many were misty eyed. In Dorothy Cave's words from *Beyond Courage*, many of the veterans, parents, and loved ones no doubt "whispered the words that sustained them—their prayer, their battle cry, their defiance of death, their buoy of hope, and their pledge of faith: 'God Bless America'." As they looked eastward, they saw 'A' Mountain bathed in sunshine. And they were overcome with pride, and their sadness turned to hope, because their thoughts were of the future. For they knew that the sons and daughters of NM A&M and America had endured and that their College and their country would prosper.

Appendix A

Last Will and Testament of William C. Porter, II

Bilibid Prison
Manila, Philippines
December 12, 1944

I, William C. Porter II, Captain U.S. Army - O-395518, being at present a prisoner of war and as such held by Japan; being in sound mental health do publish this as my last will and testament.

1. I name my mother, Mrs. William Asa Porter, now residing in the City of El Paso, Texas - U.S.A. as my sole benefactor and heiress.
2. I furthermore appoint my mother, Mrs. William Asa Porter as my executrix, with full powers of attorney.
3. I leave to my benefactor all pay, and allowances due me from the government of the U.S., all insurances, and all property, and possessions either mine or due me through inheritance.

Signed
William C. Porter

Photocopy of original William C. Porter, II will
written in Bilibid Prison prior to his being shipped out
on the *Oryoku Maru*.

Bilibid Prison
Manila, Philippines
December 12, 1944

I, William C. Porter II, Captain U.S. Army -
O-395518, being at present a prisoner of war
and as such, held by Japan; being in sound
mental health do publish this as my last
will and testament.

1. I name my mother, Mrs. William Asa
Porter, now residing in the city of El Paso,
Texas - U.S.A. as my sole benefactor and
heiress.

2. I furthermore appoint my mother, Mrs.
William ASA Porter as my executrix, with
full powers of attorney.

3. I leave to my benefactor all pay, and allowances
due me from the government of the U.S., all insurances,
and all property, and possessions either mine or due
me thru inheritance. Signed William C. Porter

Appendix B

NM AGGIES KNOWN TO HAVE BEEN CAPTURED IN THE PHILIPPINES

[Rank, Name, Last Year at NM A&M (if known), Hometown, Unit, Camp of Liberation or Death, Hell Ship]

Sgt. Robert Amy, ?, Silver City, 200th CA, Honsho Camp, Japan, ship unknown

Sgt. Ernest J. Armijo, ?, Peralta, 200th CA, Mukden, Manchuria, *Tottori Maru*

Pfc. Byron C. Beal, '39, Elida, 200th CA, died May 27, 1942 at Camp O'Donnell

Lt. Darwin C. Becker, '36, Brenham, TX; 200th CA, died of exposure 1 day after *Brazil Maru* landed at Moji; was one of 450 survivors of 1619 original POWs to arrive at Moji; died January 30, 1945 shortly after arrival

Lt. Dow Bond, ?, Albuquerque/Taos, 200th CA, Camp Rokuroshi, *Nagato Maru*

Cpl. George A. Brasuel, ?, Canyon, TX, 31st Infantry (Co. A), Camp Cabanatuan

Sgt. Lew Ira Calkins, '27, Albuquerque, 200th CA, died in POW Camp Cabanatuan, July 13, 1942

Lt. Albert Bacon Fall Chase, '37, Ruidoso, 45th Infantry Regiment (73rd Infantry Division, Philippine Army), lost on Hell Ship *Shinyo Maru*, September 7, 1944.

Sgt. Edward E. Chavez, ?, Albuquerque, 200th CA, camp and ship unknown

Sgt. William R. Coleman, ?, Hot Springs, 200th CA, Mukden Camp, ship unknown

Lt. James W. Donaldson, '37, Deming, 200th CA, Mukden, Manchuria, *Oryoku Maru*

Capt. John W. Farley, '38?, Raton, 200th CA, Kyoshu Camp, Japan, ship unknown

Lt. Pecos U. Finley, '39, Causey, Philippine Scouts QM, died at Camp O'Donnell, June 1, 1942

Sgt. John R. Flowers, '36, Lake Arthur, 200th CA, died at Camp Cabanatuan, September 11, 1942

Capt. William N. Foster, '35, Deming, Medical Detachment, Philippine Scouts, Cabanatuan, died on *Oryoku Maru*, December 15, 1944

Cpl. Evangelisto 'Evans' Garcia, ?, Doña Ana, 200th CA, Fukuoka 17, *Canadian Inventor* ship

Maj. Anthony R. George, '36, Gallup, 200th CA, Zentsuji Camp, *Tottori Maru*?

Capt. Rey F. Gonzales, '34, Mora & Lemitar, 200th CA, executed by Japanese upon arrival at O'Donnell, April 14, 1942

Capt. Gerald B. Greeman, '40, Deming, 200th CA, Mukden Camp, *Oryoku-Brazil Maru*

Pfc. Richard B. Hunt, '37, Pinos Altos, 200th CA, died on *Arisan Maru*, Oct 24, 1944

Pfc. George H. Huston, '29?, Lovington, 200th CA, died at Camp O'Donnell, May 21, 1942

Capt. Hubert P. Jeffus, '35, Lordsburg, 200th CA, died on *Arisian Maru*, October 24, 1944

Sgt. James B. Jones, ?, Albuquerque, 200th CA, POW Camp in Tokyo

Sgt. George M. Jones, '36, Lordsburg, 200th CA, died on *Arisan Maru*, October 24, 1944

Sgt. Melvin E. 'Casey' Jones, ?, Portales, 200th CA, died at Camp Cabanatuan, July 28, 1942

Sgt. Rollie H. Keller, '38?, Hope, 200th CA, Camp Nigata, ship unknown

Cpl. Robert J. Knight, ?, Carlsbad, 200th CA, Tokyo POW Camp?, *Noto Maru*

Jack S. Lewis, '40 Deming, 200th CA, Fukuoka Camp, *Canadian Inventor*

Pfc. Thomas V. 'Louie' Long, '39, Portales, 200th CA, executed at Camp Cabanatuan, August 28, 1942

Cpl. William E. Love, '40, Deming, 200th CA, died from diphtheria Camp Cabanatuan, August 24, 1942

Cpl. Robert O. Lucero, (?), Dawson, 200th CA, Camp Hitachi 1, ship unknown

Sgt. Solly Manasse, Las Cruces, '35?, 200th CA, Camp Hanawa, *Noto Maru*

Benjamin Marquez, ?, Seboyeta, no other information

Capt. John T. McCorkle, '32, Las Cruces, 4th Air Base Group, killed in action on Bataan, January 1942

Lt. Com. John R. McFie, '05, Las Cruces, killed by shell fragments at POW Camp Santo Tomas (wife Dorothy survived) during battle to retake Manila, February 3, 1945.

Sgt. Charles R. Nunn, '38?, Hillsboro, 200th CA, Mukden Camp, ship unknown

Sgt. David Maclean Nunn, '39?, Lake Valley, 200th CA, Camp unknown, ship unknown

Sgt. Arnold A. Orosco, '39, Albuquerque, 200th CA Medical Detachment, died on *Arisan Maru,* October 24, 1944

Sgt. Thomas M. Palmer, '37, Albuquerque, 200th CA Band, died just after liberation of Bilibid POW camp, Manila, February 13, 1945

Capt. William F. Porter, '41, Las Cruces, 91st Infantry Division, Mukden, Manchuria, *Oryoku Maru*

Pvt. Francis B. 'Buster' Powell, '40?, Santa Fe, 31st Infantry Division Medical Detatchment, died on *Oryoku Maru*, December 15, 1944

Lt. Robert J. Remondini, '40, Deming, 200th CA, Cabanatuan and Davao POW camps, died on *Shinyo Maru* on September 7, 1944

Pfc. William B. Richardson, ?, McDonald, NM, 200th CA, Omori 3, ship unknown

Sgt. Andrew J. 'Jiggs' Robinson, '37?, Hillsboro, 200th CA, Mukden, Manchuria, ship unknown

Lt. Lloyd W. Rogers, ?, Santa Fe or Carrizozo, 27th Bomb Group, died May 27, 1942 at Camp O'Donnell

Maj. Maynard G. Snell, College Station, TX, ex-NM A&M instructor, 192nd Tank Battalion, died on *Oryoku Maru*, December 15, 1944

Capt. Charles R. Sparks, '38, Las Cruces, 41st Infantry Division, died at Camp Cabanatuan, June 21, 1942

Lt. Joseph Dallas Thorpe, '37, Artesia, 200th CA, came to Moji on *Brazil Maru*, died of dysentery and exposure on January 27, 1945, Kyushu, Japan

Lt. William A. Trogstad, '37, Las Vegas, (unit unknown), died at Camp Cabanatuan, November 7, 1942; was in Philippines with Morrison Mining Co., went into Army and fought on Bataan; wife Martha liberated from Los Banos in February 1945

Lt. J. J. Valdenaar, ?, El Paso, (no additional information)

Sgt. Charles N. Williams, '37?, Lordsburg, 200th CA, Tokyo POW camp, *Noto Maru*

Sgt. Phil Witherspoon, ?, Artesia, 200th CA, Camp Cabanatuan?

Lt. Capshaw Wolf, ?, Miami, OK, (no additional information)

Sgt. Paul F. Womack, ?, Carlsbad, 200th CA, Tokyo POW camp?, *Noto Maru*

Sgt. Foster W. Zimmerman, '38?, Rogers, NM, 200th CA, camp unknown, ship unknown

Appendix C

NM AGGIES DEACEASED IN SERVICE IN WORLD WAR II
Rank, Name, Last Year at NM A&M, Hometown, Unit, nature of death and date.
Listed men are as documented in NMSU Archives and "War Books."
There may be more not listed here for whom records are incomplete.

Lt. Ellis J. Ackerman, '41, Deming, killed in plane cash near Cross City, Florida on November 5, 1942.

Sgt. Garland G. Alcorn, '41, Artesia, killed in action over Germany, December 1943.

Sgt. Richard F. Anderson, '36, Houston, pilot with Royal Canadian Air Force was killed over England, February 6, 1942.

Lt. Melecio Apodaca, '34, Garfield, killed in plane crash near Wayne, Nebraska, October 10, 1943.

Pfc. Bryan Armstrong, '39, House, killed in action on German front, January 1945.

Sgt. William T. Atchley, '41, Grenville, NM, killed over Eniwetok in Pacific, May 4, 1944.

Lt. Willis W. Baird, '42, Tularosa, killed in Normandy, France, June 9, 1944.

Pfc. Byron C. Beal, '39, Elida, 200th CA, died May 27, 1942 at POW Camp O'Donnell, Philippines.

William C. Beaty, '42, Las Cruces, merchant seaman killed in Atlantic, May 18, 1943.

Lt. Darwin C. Becker, '36, Brenham, TX, 200th CA, died of exposure one day after Japanese Hell Ship *Brazil Maru* landed at Moji, Japan, was among 450 survivors of original 1619 POWs to arrive, died January 30, 1945.

Seaman 2nd Class Charles L. Billups, '41, Alamogordo, killed in action in Battle of Savo Island off Guadalcanal on the cruiser *USS Astoria*, August, 1942.

Eugene Bleiler, ?, ?, killed in action in Bismark Sea, May 7, 1943

Lt. (j.g.) Joseph J. Bloch, '41, Brackenridge, PA, killed in action over the South Pacific, December 4, 1943.

Lt. Frank E. Budenholzer, '38, Belen, killed in bomber crash at Memphis, Tennessee, March 21, 1942.

Sgt. Ernesto G. Burciaga, '38, Roswell, was killed in action in Europe (date unknown).

Sgt. Francis W. Cade, '43, Las Cruces, killed in action in Germany, March 17, 1945.

Sgt. Lew I Calkins, '27, Albuquerque, 200th CA, died in POW Camp Cabanatuan, Philippines, July 13, 1942.

Pvt. Andrew B. Candelaria, '40, El Paso, killed in action in France, September 29, 1944.

Lt. Robert L. Carr, '42, Tularosa, killed in action over Japan, July 9, 1945.

James J. Carrico, ?, ? , killed in action off South Korea, June 27, 1945.

Capt. John L. Chapin, '33, El Paso, killed in action on the Italian front, January 22, 1944.

Lt. Albert Bacon Fall Chase, '37, Ruisdoso, 45th Infantry Regiment (73rd Infantry Division Philippine Army), lost on Hell Ship *Shinyo Maru*, September 7, 1944.

Sgt. Alex L. Chavez, '40, Las Cruces, killed in action over Africa, October 20, 1943.

Lt. Harold D. Colvard, '41, Oinita, OK, killed in plane crash near Chengtu, China, August 23, 1944.

Lt. Wade H. Corn, Jr., '43, Roswell, killed in action on Cebu Island, Philippines, March 29, 1945.

Lt. Joseph M. Coyle, ?, ?, killed over Viet Nam, April 28, 1945.

Cadet Angelo J. Cunico, '41, Raton, lost at sea (Gulf of Mexico) during plane accident, May 1942.

Seaman 2nd Class Frederick G. Crawford, ?, ?, killed on carrier *Liscome Bay* near Gilbert Islands, November 24, 1943.

Seaman 2nd Class Jack D. Dale, ?, ?, died from service-related injuries at San Diego Naval Hospital, February 1, 1946.

Lt. Ralph E. Davies, '41, Ft. Sumner, killed in plane crash at Plains, La., March 18, 1944.

Lt. (j.g.) Fran M. Delgado, Jr., '41, Las Vegas, killed in action in South Pacific in August 1944.

Cpl. William A. Eakens, '41, Las Cruces, killed in action on Iwo Jima, March 8, 1945.

Sgt. Robert R. Earp, '42, Grenville, NM, killed in action over Denmark, February 22, 1944.

Cadet Byron Eby, '40, Faywood, NM, killed in plane crash at Corpus Christi, July 15, 1943.

Sgt. Thomas R. Edmondson, '40, Parker, AZ, killed in action in Germany, November 16, 1944.

Lt. Leo M. Eminger, '40, Anthony, killed in B-17 over Solomon Islands, October 1942.

Lt. Pecos U. Finley, '39, Causey, Philippine Scouts Quartermaster, died in POW camp O'Donnell, Philippines, June 1, 1942.

Sgt. John R. Flowers, '36, Lake Arthur, 200th CA, died in POW Camp Cabanatuan, Philippines, September 11, 1942.

Lt. Lisle Foord, '42, Las Vegas, Marine Air Corps, killed over Vella Lavella Island in the Solomons, August, 1944.

Capt. William N. Foster, '35, Deming, Medical Detachment, Philippine Scouts, lost on Japanese Hell Ship *Oryoku Maru*, December 15, 1944.

Lt. Chris P. Fox, Jr., '41, El Paso, killed in action in Germany, February 27, 1945.

Lt. Edward D. Fuller, '41, El Paso, killed over Western Europe, February 1943.

Lt. Francis, W. Gallagher, '39, Las Cruces, killed during battle for Leyte, Philippines, November 13, 1944.

Lt. Joe H. Gardner, '37, Sierra Blanca, TX, killed in plane crash at Woods Hole, MA, March 3, 1944.

Pilot Henry G. Gilbert, Jr., '38, Lovell, WY, killed in plane battle over Rangoon, Burma, December 23, 1941.

Capt. Rey F. Gonzales, '34, Mora & Lemitar, 200th CA, executed by Japanese after Death March at POW Camp O'Donnell, Philippines, April 14, 1942.

Capt. Walter K. Goss, Jr., '41, Las Cruces, killed in plane crash in Burma, February 5, 1945.

Lt. Edward E. Gray, '40, La Mesa, killed in naval action off Okinawa, May 1945. Brother George ('32) was incarcerated at Los Banos and helped lead daring rescue of inmates by Army paratroopers in Febuary 1945.

Lt. Robert W. Gray, '41, Wheatridge, CO, killed in action in Africa, March 22, 1943.

Sgt. Frank Haggard, '40, La Jolla, CA, killed in European theatre, December 25, 1944.

Lt. Vernon D. Hall, '43, Santa Fe, killed on European front, January 15, 1945.

Lt. Choctaw A. Harp, Jr. '41, Cimarron, killed in plane crash at Lake Providence, Louisiana, May 13, 1944.

Lt. William W. Harris, '42, Tucumcari, killed in action in France, June 18, 1944.

Ensign Robert H Hedley, '40, Carlsbad, killed on ship after returning from bombing run, Luzon, Philippines, January 21, 1945.

Lt. Hans R. Heyne, '43, Mogollon, killed at Landau, Germany, October 1944.

Pvt. Otho W. Holtzclaw, '42, House, killed in action in Gilbert Islands, January 1944.

Lt. (j.g.) Marvn P. Horton, Jr., '41, Oklahoma, killed in plane crash at Alameda, CA, October 20, 1943.

Pfc. Richard B. Hunt, '37, Pinos Altos, 200th CA, lost on Japanese Hell Ship *Arisan Maru*, October 24, 1944.

Lt. Billy D. Hunter, '41, Silver City, lost in air action in South Pacific, August 1943.

Lt. Clarence E. Huston, ?, ?, killed in action over Europe, May 28, 1944.

Cpl. George H. Huston, '29?, Lovington, 200th CA, died in POW Camp O'Donnell, Philippines, May 21, 1942.

Capt. Hubert P. Jeffus, '35, Lordsburg, 200th CA, lost on Japanese Hell Ship *Arisan Maru*, October 24, 1944.

Neal K. Johnson, '42, Tucumcari, no additional information.

Sgt. George M. Jones, '36, El Paso, 200th CA, lost on Japanese Hell Ship *Arisan Maru*, October 24, 1944.

Sgt. Melvin E. 'Casey' Jones, ?, Portales, 200th CA, died in POW Camp Cabanatuan, July 28, 1942.

Franklin E. Ladd, '43, Mosquero, killed in action in Germany, April 8,1945.

Lt. Harold E. Lane, '40, Alamogordo, killed in air action over Western Europe, April 17, 1943.

Capt. Gerald E. Leach, '38, Gardner, MA, committed suicide at Camp Hood, TX.

Lt. Jack Lee, '41, Alamogordo, 13th Air Force, killed in air action at Bougainville (Solomons), November 18, 1942.

Lt. Herman W. Lewis, '40, Grady, killed in Africa, January 1943.

Lt. Col. Hampton H. Lisle, '28, Las Cruces, killed in action in Italy, April 7, 1945.

Pfc. Thomas V. 'Louie' Long, '39, Portales, 200th CA, executed by Japanese at POW Camp Cabanatuan, August 28, 1942.

Cpl. William E. Love, '40, Deming, 200th CA, died in POW Camp Cabanatuan, August 24, 1942.

Capt. William R. Ludwig, '40, Albuquerque, killed in action in Italy, November 18, 1944.

Lt. Don W. Lusk, Jr. '41, Silver City, killed in action over Western Europe, January 3, 1943.

Lt. Col. Jesse Mechem, '33, Las Cruces, 96th Infantry Division, killed in action on Leyte, Philip pines, October 29, 1944.

Capt. John R. McCorkle, '32, Las Cruces, 4th Air Base Group, killed in action on Bataan, January 1942.

Lt. Com. John R. McFie, '05, Las Cruces, killed by shell fragments at POW Camp Santo Tomas (wife Dorothy survived) during battle to retake Manila, February 3, 1945.

Sgt. Charles D. McGinley, '40, Monahans, TX, killed in action over New Ireland (South Pacific), April 28, 1944.

Lt. Paul McLaughlin, '41, Hatch, killed in action over Central Pacific, January 22, 1944.

Capt. J. Laverne Nicklas, '35, Portales, killed in action in Germany, April 16, 1945.

Sgt. Arnold A. Orosco, '39, Albuquerque, 200th CA, lost on Hell Ship *Arisan Maru*, October 24, 1944.

Lt. Ralph P. Ortiz, '42, Santa Fe, lost over Ellice Island in Central Pacific, January 1944.

Cpl. Robert Ortiz, '40?, El Paso, 5th Marine Div., killed in action on Iwo Jima, March 1, 1945.

Sgt. Thomas M. Palmer, '37, 200th CA Band, Albuquerque, died just after release from POW Camp Bilibid, Manila, Philippines, February 13, 1945.

Sgt. Joseph F. Parks, '42, Lake Valley, killed over Europe March 25, 1945.

Pvt. Francis B. 'Buster' Powell, ?, Garfield, 31st Infantry Division (Philippines), died on Hell Ship *Oryoku Maru*, December 15, 1944.

Lt. Henry Provencio, ?, ?, killed in air action in Pacific, December 25, 1944.

Lt. James S. Quesenberry, '41, lost over South Pacific, May 1944.

Lt. Wilmer E. Ragsdale, '29, Artesia, killed in Navy plane fire near Boston, MA, July 10, 1945.

Capt. James F. Redford, '37, Hot Springs/El Paso, killed in action in Europe, December 11, 1944.

Capt. Oren R. Reichelt, '41, Strauss, NM, killed in action in France, July 3, 1944.

Lt. Robert J. Remondini, '40, Deming, 200th CA, lost on Hell Ship *Arisan Maru*, October 24, 1944.

Lt. Joseph L. Resley, '41, Las Cruces, killed in plane crash near San Francisco, November 30, 1944.

Willam B. Richardson, ?, McDonald, NM, 200th CA, died at POW Camp Omori, Japan.

Lt. L.W. Rogers, ?, Santa Fe, 27th Bomber Group (Philippines), died in POW Camp O'Donnell, May 17, 1942.

Lt. George L. Salazar, '41, Springer, killed in action on German front, November 16, 1944.

Lt. Reese Savelle, '40, Berino, killed in plane crash at Woodland, WA, December 2, 1943.

Sgt. Herman Sedillo, ?, ?, died at Beaumont Hospital in El Paso, July 21, 1945.

Sgt. Robert T. Shields, '38, San Bernardino, CA, US Marines, died of wounds received in action during landing at Leyte, Phillipines, October 20, 1944.

Capt. Lee Silbo, '43, Farmington, lost over Atlantic, June 17, 1945.

Capt. John M. Silva, '27, Clint, TX, killed in plane crash in China, March 11, 1944.

Lt. Roy W. Skipworth, '41, Ft. Sumner, killed in action on Okinawa, April 5, 1945.

Maj. Maynard G. Snell, ex-NM A&M instructor, Bryan, TX, lost on Hell Ship *Oryoku Maru*, December 15, 1944.

Cpl. Rodney R. Sorenson, ?, ?, killed in Chengtu China, January 19, 1945.

Capt. Charles R. Sparks, '38, Las Cruces, 41st Division (Philippine), died in POW Camp Cabanatuan, Philippines, June 21, 1942.

Lt. William J. Spence, '40, El Paso, killed in Southwest Pacific, May 20, 1944.

Lt. Frank D. Taylor, '44, ?, killed in action at Wurzburg, Germany, April 24, 1945.

Cadet Fred G. Thayer, '41, Carlsbad, killed in plane accident at Williams, AZ, March 14, 1943.

Lt. Robert C. Thompson, '43, Santa Fe, killed in plane crash at Alexandria, LA, March 19, 1944.

Lt. Dallas Thorpe, '37, Artesia, 200th CA, died in Kyushu, Japan soon after arriving on Hell Ship *Brazil Maru*, January 27, 1945.

Lt. James Toliver, '41, Vaughn, killed in bombing raid over Tokyo, February 1945.

Lt. William A. Trogstad, '37, Las Vegas, served on Bataan (unit unknown) died in POW Camp Cabanatuan, November 7, 1942. Was in Philippines with Morrison Mining Co., wife Marha liberated from POW Camp Los Banos, February 1945.

Lt. Col. John P. Usher, '30, Ponoma, KS, killed in action in Luxembourg, October 7, 1943.

Lt. Placido Vigil, Jr., '40, Espanola, killed in plane crash in Gulf of Mexico, May 24, 1944.

Lt. Vincent A. Van Dersarl, '41, Raton, killed in action over Burma, December 9, 1944.

Capt. Frank L. Wayne, '26, Alamogordo, killed in auto accident at Dorchester, England, June 24, 1944.

Brig. General James E. Wharton, '17, Staunton, VA, killed in action in France, August 12, 1944.

Lt. (j.g.) James M. Wilkerson, '41, Quay, killed in plane crash in Hawaii, June 30, 1943.

Robert J. Williams, '36, Canutillo, TX, died in Beaumont Hospital, El Paso, January 14, 1943.

Harvey D. Williamson, '38, Stigler, OK, killled in action in Philippines, April 29, 1942.

Cadet Elbert E. Wood, '43, Fort Sumner, killed in plane crash near Stanton, TX, December 27, 1944.

Lt. Speegle J. Wood, '41, Sweetwater, TX, killed in auto accident at Montrose, GA, May 4, 1942.

Capt. Warren M. Wright, '40, 5th Marine Div., killed in action on Iwo Jima, February 24, 1945.

Lt. Delmar Yenzer, '42, Crescent, OK, killed in action at Normandy, June 13, 1944.

Lt. Ted E. Zavilla, '43, Magdalena, killed in action in Germany, April 15, 1945.

SELECTED BIBLIOGRAPHY

Alcine, Cpl. Bill, *"Landing on Los Negros"* — in *The Best From Yank, The Army Weekly*. Cleveland: The World Publishing Co., 1945.

Breuer, William B., *Retaking the Philippines: America's Return to Corregidor and Bataan*. New York: St. Martin's Press, 1986.

Cave, Dorothy, *Beyond Courage: One Regiment Against Japan*. Las Cruces: Yucca Tree Press, 1992.

Dyess, William E., *The Dyess Story: The Eye Witness Account of the Death March from Bataan and the Narrative of Experiences in Japan*. New York: C. P. Putnam's Sons, 1944.

Flanagan, Lt. Gen. E. M., Jr., *Corregidor: The Rock Force Assault*. Novato, CA: Presidio Press, 1988.

Greenfield, Kent R., ed., *The War Against Japan: U.S. Army in World War II, Pictorial Record*. Washington, D.C: U.S. Army, 1952

Griffin, Marcus and Matson, Eva Jane, *Heroes of Bataan, Corregidor and Northern Luzon, 2nd ed*. Las Cruces: Yucca Tree Press, 1994.

Hammel, Eric, *Guadalcanal: Starvation Island*. New York: Crown Publishers, 1987.

Hartendorp, A.V.H., *The Santo Tomas Story*. New York: McGraw-Hill Book Co., 1964.

Karig, Captain Walter and Purdon, Commander Eric, *Battle Report: Pacific War Middle Phase*. New York: Rinehart and Co., Inc., 1947.

Katcher, Philip, *U.S. 1st Marine Division: 1941-1945*. London: Osprey Publishing Co., 1986.

Knox, Donald, *Death March: The Survivors of Bataan*. New York: Harcourt Brace Jovanovich, 1981.

Kropp, Simon F., Ph.D., *That All May Learn*. Las Cruces: New Mexico State Univ., 1972.

MacArthur, Douglas, *Reminiscences*. New York, McGraw-Hill Book Co., 1964.

Manchester, William, *American Caesar*. Boston: Little, Brown and Co., 1978.

McAulay, Lex, *Battle of the Bismarck Sea*: New York: St. Martin's Press, 1991

Matson, Eva Jane, *It Tolled For New Mexico*. Las Cruces: Yucca Tree Press, 1994.

Michener, James A., *Tales of the South Pacific*. New York: Fawcett Crest, 1946.

Morton, Lewis, *The Fall of the Philippines*. Washington, D.C.: U.S. Army Center of Military History, 1953.

Mydans, Carl, "My God! It's Carl Mydans," in *Life Magazine*, Vol. 18, No. 8: Feb. 19, 1945.

Posz, Joseph D., *Military Heroes of New Mexico Military Institute*. Roswell, NM: McBride Museum, NMMI, 1994.

Ross, Bill D., *Peleliu Tragic Triumph*: New York: Random House, 1991.

Schultz, Duane, *Hero of Bataan: The Story of General Jonathan M. Wainwright*. New York: St. Martin's Press, 1981.

Smith, Robert R., *The Approach to the Philippines: The War in the Pacific*. Washington, D.C., U.S. Army Center of Military History, 1953.

Steinberg, Rafael, *Return to the Philippines*. Chicago: Time-Life Books, 1979.

Steinberg, Rafael, *Island Fighting*. Chicago: Time-Life Books, 1979.

Taylor, Michael F., *Aggies, Oh Aggies, or The Glory Years: New Mexico A&M, 1935-1939.* (Unpublished memoir), Carlsbad, NM, 1978.

Thomas, Edward E., *As I Remember:* E. E. Thomas, Sonoita, AZ, 1990.

Thomas, Gerald W., *Torpedo Squadron Four: A Cockpit View of World War II.* Las Cruces, NM: Rio Grande Historical Collections, New Mexico State Univ., 1990.

Thomas, Gerald W., et al (eds.), *Victory in World War II: The New Mexico Story.* Las Cruces, NM: New Mexico State Univ., 1994.

Van Sickle, Emily, *The Iron Gates of Santo Tomas.* Chicago: Chicago Academy Press, 1992.

Wheeler, Keith, *The Road to Tokyo.* Chicago: Time-Life Books, 1979.

Young, Donald J., *The Battle of Bataan.* Jefferson, NC: McFarland & Co., 1992.

INDEX

165